Additional Praise for the First Edition

"Miller's work is not only empowering for those who have a vision for growth, it is also very helpful for those who are seasoned and experienced in ministry. I recommend it to everyone."
— Rev. William D. Watley, Ph.D., pastor,
St. James AME Church, Newark, New Jersey

"This book consistently helps pastors empower laity while maintaining appropriate pastoral leadership. It is also deeply spiritual while providing a solid theological undergirding and a scriptural mandate for the practical work of administration and leadership."
— Dr. Edward L. Wheeler, president,
Christian Theological Seminary, Indianapolis

"A must-read for pastors and church ministry leaders looking for help in their administration of the church. Miller offers administrative advice and suggests methods that not only explain what to do, but show an implementation process for accomplishing statistical growth."
— Dr. Roscoe D. Cooper, Jr., pastor,
Metropolitan African American Baptist Church,
Richmond, Virginia; past general secretary,
National Baptist Convention USA, Inc.

"God's how-to plan for church growth. Miller has given the instructive path to anyone who talks about church growth. Read it and walk your talk."   — Rev. Dr. Cecil L. "Chip" Murray, pastor emeritus,
First AME Church, Los Angeles

"*Go Grow Your Church!* is a book that most pastors in the African American church tradition have been waiting for! In addition to providing some much-needed "how-tos" in the practical areas of ministry, Miller gives essential step-by-step instructions for constructing a spiritual foundation for the lives of both pastors and parishioners."
— Rev. Dr. Jeremiah A. Wright Jr., retired senior pastor,
Trinity United Church of Christ, Chicago

GO GROW YOUR CHURCH!

SPIRITUAL LEADERSHIP FOR
AFRICAN AMERICAN CONGREGATIONS

JAMES F. MILLER

FOREWORD BY
VASHTI MURPHY MCKENZIE

THE
PILGRIM
PRESS
Cleveland

The Pilgrim Press
700 Prospect Avenue
Cleveland, Ohio 44115-1100
thepilgrimpress.com

Library of Congress Cataloging-in-Publication Data

Miller, James F., 1953–
    Go grow your church! : spiritual leadership for African American
  congregations / James F. Miller ; foreword by Vashti Murphy McKenzie.
      p. cm.
  Includes bibliographical references.
  ISBN-13: 978-0-8298-1801-7 (alk. paper)
  1. African American churches. 2. Church growth. 3. Christian leadership.
  I. Title.
  BR563.N4M53 2008
  253.089′96073 – dc22

                                            2008014340

1 2 3 4 5 6 7 8 9 10   14 13 12 11 10 09 08

Contents

Foreword

At last! This will be the sigh of relief that comes from both pulpit and pew when people read *Go Grow Your Church!* by Dr. James Miller. The book takes into account the leader who hears from God and articulates God's will and work. It is also cognizant of the people who are molded and shaped by diverse experiences who were not in on the original conversation.

Go Grow Your Church! is a body of material that does not separate spiritual growth from an administrative managerial process. The candid sharing of experiences and research will be appreciated by those beginning the journey of ministry leadership and the mature minister looking for fresh insights.

In the mid-1990s, Bishop Frederick Calhoun James was the presiding prelate of the Second Episcopal District of the African Methodist Episcopal Church, where I served as pastor of Payne Memorial AME Church in Baltimore. He sponsored a trip to southern Africa and encouraged those who could to join him in the places where he had served as the Episcopal servant.

Joining the preachers and people of the Second District were several from the Fourth District, which included the state of Illinois. Among them were Presiding Elder Roy Miller and his son, Rev. James Miller. The transatlantic trip was taxing on the body for those who thought they were young. For the very mature, like Presiding Elder Miller, it had to be challenging. Yet the elder Miller never complained. The younger Miller was attentive and sensitive to the needs of his father.

It was during this trip that I met the Millers. The father was very engaging. He was a fountain of stories, which we all enjoyed. His son was a quiet presence who helped his father navigate over and around the Maluti Mountains of Lesotho.

Under the quiet exterior of the Rev. James Miller was the explosive power of the Holy Spirit already set in motion to build God's church and God's people. Many years later, when given the opportunity to preach at the incredible DuPage AME Church outside of Chicago, I saw with my own eyes and felt in my own spirit the special calling upon the life of James and Lana Miller.

Presiding Elder Roy has found a resting place in eternity, but his wit and wisdom are still alive in his son's book *Go Grow Your Church!*

Dr. Miller shares the transitional story of taking DuPage AME from a church shocked at pastoral transition and looking for a new church home to a church with a building program that accommo-dated the needs of the people. There is a plethora of stories that show how God met them at every turn and led them through the search for a building, buying property, worshiping in a hotel, to finally building a new place.

Everyone wants a growing church. Everyone doesn't always count the cost of handling growing pains. Dr. Miller shares the why and the how of his wrestling with what God wanted and what he wanted.

In the chapters that follow, Dr. Miller shares that one of the keys to evangelism is how visitors are handled. The Closed Network Evange-lism, or CBE, shows how prospective members are cultivated through normal daily activities. He uses the scriptural imperative of the Great Commission (Matt. 28:19) to encourage worshipers to share the good news of Christ and the Sunday bulletin. The first is obvious. It is the personal testimony of people who have encountered Christ in wor-ship. The second is not so obvious. The bulletin is both an invitation and a description of the church that cannot be shared in casual con-versation. The result is an increase in the number of visitors, which equals an increase of potential members.

In order for this outreach to be effective, visitors must be docu-mented and a deliberate response or follow-up must be instituted. Membership classes taught by pastors are critical.

The author keeps in mind the voluntary nature of the church. People invest their treasure but also their emotional and physical selves. Dr. Miller understands that a person who is growing in grace and godliness realizes that blessings can come in unexpected ways that we can never anticipate. The testimony of DuPage's growth affirms that God moves in unexpected and exciting ways toward a divinely inspired conclusion.

Dr. Miller uses a total church teaching modality that immerses the congregation in the subject or issue from every point of view, including printed material, Bible study, and worship. He emphasizes that the fiscal key to effective stewardship is a strategic approach to how the financial resources are raised.

Go Grow Your Church! provides insights not only on evangelism and stewardship but also on raising the church budget, planning capital projects, financing capital projects, worship, and personal and congregational spiritual growth.

He concludes with "Seven Paths to Your Best Ministry Now!" This chapter highlights priorities for all pastors and ministry leaders. They include the need to develop a spiritual perspective on life and ministry that must be maintained by practicing spiritual discipline. This will help a person to maintain good spiritual health. In order for the important things to be done, leaders must prioritize in ministry. The temptation is to be busy, but busy does not equal blessed.

Dr. Miller stresses that in order to grow a church there is a need to develop disciplined people with disciplined thoughts and actions. This will require the maintenance of a self-care discipline.

Love creates the adhesive that bonds the uniqueness of individuals into the body of Christ. Dr. Miller indicates that in order to "wage peace" in the midst of conflict, love becomes the weapon to win souls for Christ. Courtesy and kindness must be expressed at every opportunity.

Finally, he notes that the ministry leader must cultivate patience with understanding and an acceptance of God's will in every circumstance.

As I think back to those three weeks during which we explored South Africa and Lesotho together with a motley crew of clergy and laity, I realize that Dr. Miller was demonstrating his approach to ministry. He expressed kindness, quietly undergirding our African sojourn. He met the challenge of travel with a sweet disposition. He helped us all become more of a family even though we were from different places and experiences.

This book is a valuable resource that can be used for instruction and training for clergy and lay leadership. It will be useful for individual study as well as for groups of students preparing to be instruments of the Most High God in building and growing people, communities, and congregations. Enjoy!

Vashti Murphy McKenzie
August 2008

Preface

On October 14, 1989, at St. Stephen AME Church in Detroit, Bishop J. Haskell Mayo, who then presided over the district in which I serve, appointed me to the pastorate of DuPage. Handing me the appointment, he looked at me and Rev. Lana Miller, who is my wife and partner in ministry, saying, "Go and build a church!" At that time we had no knowledge of the congregational life or needs of DuPage.

We did not know that this suburb west of Chicago had only a 2 percent African American population, which is our church's primary evangelistic market. We did not know that the 150-member congregation was worshiping in an old chapel-like building and had outgrown its 75-person seating capacity. We did not know that the congregation had begun efforts to purchase, rather than construct, a new church home. And we did not know that God had already set a plan in motion — a plan that would result in congregational increase, facility expansion, and spiritual growth beyond what we could ever have imagined.

We arrived at DuPage the next Sunday also not knowing that the congregation had not been prepared to receive a new pastor. Many of them did not know that the previous pastor was no longer assigned there. As we were excitedly experiencing our first day of a new opportunity, many church members were sitting and looking at me and saying, in the colloquial words of Bishop Robert Thomas Jr., "Who he?" I discovered later that many of them thought I was a guest speaker. This presented our first challenge, which was to make a pastoral connection with the people. Our efforts in this area initiated a long season of healing and reconciliation. This was needed because of the trauma the congregation experienced through this abrupt transition.

As for the directive to "build a church," the congregation was actively perusing the market of available, completed, for-sale church buildings. I learned in seminary "as a new pastor, you may change everything in six months or a year, but don't change anything in the first six weeks." This is a debatable approach to pastoral transition but in our first weeks at DuPage, its wisdom served us well. The congregation was experiencing a transitional trauma and some felt that their new pastoral family was being thrust upon them. This created some anxiety in the church.

Alvin Toffler, on page 2 of his book *Future Shock,* defines the title as "the shattering stress and disorientation that we experience by being subjected to too much change in too short a time." If I had changed the direction of the congregation at that time, it would have resulted in a backlash of congregational frustration from the increased transitional trauma. If I had removed and replaced any officers to empower a group favorable to my positions, then a confrontational relationship between pastor and congregation would have resulted. This would have hampered future ministerial efforts. If I had immediately changed the worship, the same result would have occurred again. These changes would have fueled congregational resentment by sending the message "You have been doing things the wrong way and you don't know what you are doing." In a congregation made fragile by unnerving incidents, such actions can be destructive. My father, Presiding Elder Roy L. Miller, who was sixty-six years in the Christian ministry, often said, "The pastor can't change everything. Some people the Lord has to move and some lessons the Lord has to teach. Always save something for the Lord to do."

"Too much internal conflict signals a need to 'wage peace' rather than promote change."[1] DuPage had a need for leadership intervention in several specific areas, but I proceeded with humility and constraint. Our building program, our worship, and our music department required immediate attention. Our ministerial staff and official board needed pastoral direction. I readily admit that I was not perfect in addressing all of these concerns. In some meetings, God's work would have fared better if I had done more listening and less talking. But by the grace of God and the kindness of the people, we made advancements for God's Realm.

There is a theological disclaimer regarding the building of any church. People don't build churches, God does. The Bible is very clear on this matter. Psalm 127:1 states, "Unless the Lord builds the house, those who build it labor in vain." Matthew 16:18 says, "...on this rock I will build my church." First Corinthians 3:6 says, "I planted, Apollos watered, but God gave the growth." When we speak of the construction of a church edifice or the growth of a ministry in any form, it is first and foremost the result of God's favor bestowed upon the ministry. Ministers and church members must take care in saying "I" or "we" built the church. God built the church; we simply partnered with God in its building.

The humble offerings in this book are the testimonies of how we worked with God in the building of our ministry at DuPage. My prayer is that the record of the following pages will assist others in their ministerial partnership with God.

Acknowledgments

My mother, Dr. Evelyn Laverne Miller, and my dad, Rev. Dr. Roy L. Miller, were the inspirations for the spiritual perspective that forms the theological context of my writing. My mother-in-law and father-in-law, Cleo and Rev. Lyman Parks, exemplified the practical framework of ministry that this book attempts to communicate. My brother, Roy, and sister, Eunice, along with my extended family, have given me the divine, agape love that is my heart's proof of God's reality.

I thank God for the privilege of pastoring DuPage AME Church, which continues to be a vessel for divine revelation and a model for optimizing local church resources. I praise God for the African Methodist Episcopal Church, which is giving me the opportunity to become the servant God desires me to be. The union of our connection is most certainly where hope springs eternal and the prayers of the righteous have availed much.

I am grateful for the most capable and supportive administrative staff that any leader could hope for: Morgan Dixon, Connie Brown, Alicia Rupert, Nicollé McKee (who processed all my edits), and Dr. Charles Sweet. Finally, my children, Jimal, Morgan (without whose technical expertise this book would not have been possible), Ashley, and Preston, are the special treasures whom God entrusted me with. And thank you, Lana, my wife, partner in ministry, enduring love, and faithful friend. Your support has made the difference in my doing my best in this effort.

Bless the name of God!

Introduction

I HAVE A CONFESSION TO MAKE. I never wanted to be a pastor. I didn't run from the call when it came. The thought of becoming a pastor just never occurred to me. While growing up in the church as the son of a pastor, I was never pressured or teased about going into the ministry. When I graduated from high school, my only ambition was to graduate from college and become a successful professional in some reputable profession.

As I became a young adult in the late 1970s, I worked a corporate job and enjoyed a very active social life. I was perfectly happy being a person who went to church only sporadically. My life consisted of working by day and partying by night — and I do mean practically every night.

I was quite a "party animal," who spent the day searching out places to go after work and seldom got more than four hours of sleep on any night. In those years I was living a shameful life of revelry, which was a life of sin. And, regretfully, I was very comfortable in my sin. I rationalized my sin and I justified my sin. After all, I wasn't hurting anybody.

In the spring of 1982, a nagging truth began to invade my conscience. I was hurting people. I was hurting my family, who were praying for me to fulfill the positive, constructive potential of my life. I was hurting my friends, who were afraid for my health and safety. I was hurting my professional associates, who wondered if my "partying priorities" were a detriment to our business. I was hurting myself by pursuing selfish satisfactions that were physically debilitating. I began to reflect upon my Christian upbringing and realized another truth so shocking that I felt like I had been dunked in cold water. If there was a God and a heaven, and I certainly believed that there was, then my eternal soul was in danger.

I saw my pitiable condition and realized that I was being fooled by the devil. The cunning enemy of God was deceiving me into throwing away my life and hurting the people who cared about me. I sought God in prayer. I prayed fervent prayers of repentance for several months, but it seemed that my prayers were of no avail. I felt hopelessly lost and unable to change my wasteful way of living.

On the Wednesday before Thanksgiving of that year, at approximately 9:00 a.m., I sat at my desk at work and prayed this prayer, "Lord, I learned in Sunday school about how you saved David, Daniel, Saul, and many others. From the days of my youth, I have listened to the testimonies of the saints in church. If you could do it for those persons, please do it for me." I cannot recall anything about this prayer that was different from my other prayers. I only know that after praying, I heard an audible voice of God. It was as if a person was standing behind me and speaking in my ear. I heard God clearly saying, "Go into your boss's office and confess your sins."

In all honesty, this was the last thing that I wanted to do. How could I tell the sordid truth about my life to my boss? He was not even a close personal friend. I don't know how I did it, but I was immediately obedient to God's word. I did as God instructed. It was not an easy thing to do, but I was resolved to be obedient. What I didn't know was that I was about to be fired from my job. My irresponsible behavior had caused my job performance to suffer. As I sat talking to my boss, his telephone rang. It was the human resources department and they were informing him that I should be let go. Fortunately, however, since I had begun discussing my problems with him before the phone call, instead of being fired I was released with a generous benefits package because of some procedural technicality. The company was under some legal obligation to support employees experiencing adverse personal problems, which made me immune to termination. The benefits package provided me with six months of income — enough time to correct a lot of my self-inflicted personal, legal, and financial damage. If I had waited five minutes to obey God's voice, my recovery would have been uncertain and my life would have been much more difficult. I praise God today for the miracle that saved me.

God began to lead me out of the wilderness of my life. This was the moment in my life when I committed myself to "cease to do evil and learn to do good" (Isa. 1:16b, 17a). This was my conversion experience.

I returned to church and began attending regularly. As I worshiped, the Holy Spirit would come upon me with power. I had been in church all of my life but had never experienced this dynamic presence of God. It felt like an overwhelming weight was upon me. It literally caused me to physically bend over in my seat and weep. I grieved thinking of how the adversary of God had cursed my life. I had been wonderfully blessed as a child, but as a young adult I had experienced such misery. God was showing me the horrors of spiritual warfare and calling me into the Christian ministry. God wanted me to enlist in the battle against this evil. This was my call to preach the saving grace of Jesus Christ. I accepted God's call.

The burden in my spirit to share the good news of the gospel of Jesus Christ has never been lifted. Through God's divine providence, my business training has been an asset to my ministry. My labors have primarily been in the congregational setting of local church ministry. My personal theology emphasizes repentance, conversion, and spiritual growth. Cultivating a personal relationship with God through the regular practice of spiritual disciplines is the foundation of spiritual growth. I believe that these basic Christian life applications supersede all other religious activities in facilitating our spiritual growth.

The purpose of this book is to help pastors and ministry leaders in their administration of the church. The late Rev. Louis Rawls, then pastor of Christian Tabernacle Missionary Baptist Church in Chicago, would often lend his large sanctuary to our bishops for the closing service of the Chicago AME Annual Conference. I once heard him say, "As pastors, we don't fall down so often on preaching. We fall down on administration." I have found that preaching is the great joy of pastoring and that administration is the great challenge. In this book, I will deal primarily with administration.

The ministry of this book is to offer administrative advice and suggest methods that will not only explain what to do, but also

SPIRITUAL PRACTICE MAKES SPIRITUAL PERFECTION

Daily Prayer

- ✝ Private (in your home or where the spirit leads)
- ✝ Public (at church, restaurants, family gatherings)

Bible Study

- ✝ Private (daily, in your home or where the spirit leads)
- ✝ Public (at Sunday Church School or other group settings; Wednesday Bible Study, 7:15 p.m.)

Periodic Fasting

- ✝ Private (as God leads you)
- ✝ Public (with the church body every Wednesday, in the way God leads you)

Regular Worship

- ✝ Public (EVERY SUNDAY)
- ✝ Private (in your home on a regular basis or for special occasions)

Mission

- ✝ Active participation in Christian outreach ministry (using the gifts God gave you, working where God places you)

Tithing

- ✝ 10 percent of the first fruits belong to GOD. Don't forget the stewardship of time and talent.

If my people, who are called by my name,
will humble themselves and pray
and seek my face and turn from their wicked ways,
then will I hear from heaven and will forgive their sin
and will heal their land.
2 Chronicles 7:14

show an implementation process for accomplishing the stated purpose. What distinguishes this book from the myriad of other treatises on this subject is that it takes how the congregation will respond to these methods into consideration. In the Bible, the people of God are described as being "stiff-necked" and "peculiar." In contemporary society they are busy, preoccupied, and always opinionated. Any advice on directing God's people must be sensitive to who they are. Having a good idea of what to do in the church is quite different from getting that longtime church member who is set in his or her ways to accept and support that idea. That young executive in the church who is trained in a certain way of working will not adjust his or her approach simply because the pastor has a vision. The acceptance and support of ministry initiatives by the congregation is crucial to success. Common wisdom says, "It's not what you do but how you do it." Both what to do and how to do it will be addressed in this book.

A management style that appropriates corporate management strategies, while blending them with both progressive and traditional ministry concepts, is how a successful administrative model can be developed. Progressive church administration from the perspective of dealing with God's people will be this book's theme.

Encouraging personal spiritual growth has been the cornerstone of my ministry. In this writing I will join spiritual growth with the practical aspects of church ministry. When spirituality is highlighted in the absence of a practical context, we err in ministerial application. Such theology, when it is practiced, denies the very essence of the Christ event. Christ was "born in human likeness" (Phil. 2:7b). Spiritual priorities must be synthesized with practical applications in order for authentic Christian ministry to occur. This affirms the mystery of Christ, that he was "fully God and fully [human]." Much of what I present will be drawn from our ministry at DuPage AME Church (hereafter simply referred to as DuPage). DuPage has been the congregational laboratory for these divine experiments of Christian ministry.

This book will also have theological and philosophical overtones. These will afford it a personal distinction and an ecumenical embrace. Hopefully, its contents will be applicable to other congregational and ministerial settings. You, as the reader, can appropriate the portions that will benefit your particular situation. Isaiah 9:7a says, "His authority shall grow continually." It is my prayer that this reading will result in an increase in the spiritual priorities of your life and in the lives of those to whom God has called you to minister. I also pray that you will experience a statistically quantifiable improvement and increase in the growth of your ministry.

ONE

Evangelism

While I was with them, I protected them in your name that you have given me. I guarded them, and not one of them was lost.

— JOHN 17:12A

Inspired to be Deliberate

For I am longing to see you so that I may share with you some spiritual gift to strengthen you. — ROMANS 1:11

SHORTLY BEFORE MY PASTORAL APPOINTMENT to DuPage, the Rt. Rev. Frank M. Reid II, who was then my bishop, asked me, "Miller, what do you do with your visitors?" This inquiry addressed the intentionality that is necessary for a successful evangelism process.[1] I was serving as pastor to another congregation at the time. The honest answer was that we did very little with our visitors. Other than a cursory acknowledgment during worship, there was no celebration or follow-up on visitors. This revelation of how visitors are greeted and registered is fundamental to authentic celebration and dynamic church growth.[2] This moment of convicting revelation resulted in the development of "Closed Net Evangelism" (CNE).

CNE is a simple process of cultivating prospective church members through a natural evangelistic outreach. In the course of our normal daily activities, we come in contact with an abundance of prospects for church membership. We don't have to look for new church members among strangers. They are already within the realm of our acquaintance. Every day we see people in stores, banks, schools, and everywhere we go who would be blessed by receiving an invitation to attend church. Our family, friends, and co-workers are often prime

candidates for salvation. The gospel is spread primarily through relationships. The most effective evangelism strategy is first to try to
reach those with whom you already have something in common.[3]
I heard a preacher once say, "If the church members could just get
every person in their households to come to worship, every church
would be overflowing in attendance."

Before I outline this simple but challenging process, I must mention
that when you are issuing an invitation to come to church, you must
have something to invite a person to. I am speaking of the worship
itself and the worshiping congregation. Chapter 7 will address the
dynamics of worship and the fellowshiping life of the church.

Inviting Persons to Worship

As you have sent me into the world, so I have sent them into the world.
                                                          — JOHN 17:18

At DuPage we encourage members and service attendees in their responsibility for evangelistic outreach. This is a scriptural imperative
for all believers. "Go therefore and make disciples of all nations"
(Matt. 28:19a). The inherent obligation for all Christians is to share
the good news of Jesus Christ. Worshipers are instructed to take their
bulletin with them and to carry it on their person throughout the
week. The bulletin is the most informative and the most underuti-
lized tool of evangelism in the church ministry. It tells more about
the church at a glance than can be said in much conversation.

Worshipers are told that during the course of the week, God will
bring someone across their path who is a candidate for outreach. They
will not have to search because God will reveal the person to them
very readily. It may be a co-worker, a neighbor, a family member, or
someone standing in front of them as they check out their groceries,
but it will be revealed and they will know it.

The first challenge of faith for church members who want the
church to grow is to share their bulletins, as God leads them, and
invite the person or persons to church. It may be done with an inquiry like "Do you live in this community?" or "Do you have a church
home?" They may strike up a conversation around any topic or they

EVANGELISM SHARING

*Most churches grow by word of mouth invitations
to family, friends, and acquaintances.*

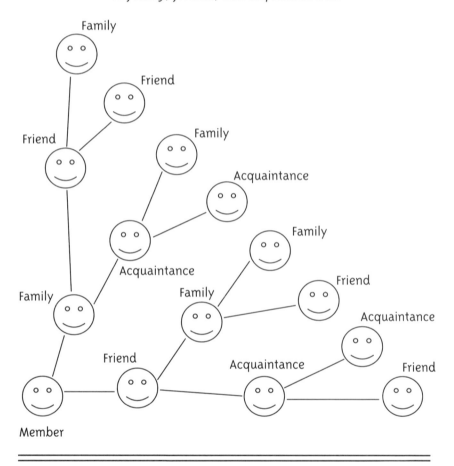

may just say, "Excuse me, I just wanted to share my church bulletin with you and invite you to worship with us." It could happen in any number of ways. The point is that the people God wants to bring into the house of prayer are all around us all the time. God calls Christians to exercise faith and to let the Holy Spirit work through that faith to the salvation of souls. Bill Hybels, senior pastor of Willow

Creek Church in Barrington, Illinois, simply encourages Christians to "walk across the room." Having the courage and the conviction to broach the topic of Christ builds our faith and raises the spiritual awareness of people around us. This initiative, like those of any organization, must be managed and promoted for it to have a consistently optimal effect. A constant encouragement in this endeavor is necessary to ensure that this process of evangelism remains a part of the congregation's ongoing culture.

Hospitality to Worshipers

And may the Lord make you increase and abound in love for one another and for all, just as we abound in love for you.
                                                    — 1 THESSALONIANS 3:12

When the CNE process is consistently encouraged and followed, there will be an increase in the number of weekly visitors. The next step in evangelism is hospitality. Genuine caring is the engine in each local church that propels growth.[4] There is nothing worse for a visitor than to come into a church for the first time and feel like a stranger. A visitor should always be welcomed like a family member who is returning home after a long journey. What should never happen is for a visitor to leave the church, saying, "I was there for two hours and no one spoke to me." As Christians we are engaged in spiritual warfare. It is intimidating for the average person to visit a church for the first time. There is a natural anxiety about being in unfamiliar territory and this anxiety is greater for a first time church visitor. The church members have the responsibility to make visitors feel welcome and at home. The persons who are attending church have come to worship, and the worship experience does not begin with the liturgical "call to worship." "Worship begins with a sense of warmth, and warmth begins in the parking lot."[5] DuPage has always been known for its warm greeting of visitors. This greeting begins at curbside or in the parking lot. Our hospitality ministry has now evolved to include a ministry of parking attendance hosts, foyer hosts (greeters), and, of course, the traditional sanctuary hosts (ushers).[6]

When it is visitor recognition time during worship, I believe it is better to let the visitors introduce themselves. This may not be logistically feasible in some churches, depending on the sanctuary size and other factors. Some think that this makes visitors feel uncomfortable. I think that there is a special witness and power in a person's voice being heard in God's house. It might also help them to feel more a part of the church. A visitor's sense of belonging and ownership in a church can begin with an opportunity for them to speak. Even those who are most shy can gain some spiritual esteem from it. We ask the first-time visitors to stand and not only to introduce themselves, but also tell who they are with, or how they came to be with us. This not only allows the visitors to be celebrated but also celebrates the faithful disciple who brought or invited them. In their book *The Five-Star Church*, Stan Toler and Adam Nelson say, "Celebrate whatever you want to see more of."[7] We certainly want to see more visitors. Visitors are prospective church members. The more visitors that we see, the more new members we will have. The visitor's expressions also perform an ongoing survey of which outreaches are being effective. The reasons for visitor's church attendance range from invitations of the most intimate of family members or friends to "I found you in the Yellow Pages."

Visitor Documentation and Response

He who is faithful in a very little is faithful also in much; and whoever is dishonest in a very little is also dishonest in much.   — LUKE 16:10

We ask the visitors to be seated after each individual introduction. After the last visitor has spoken and sat down, the congregation stands and sings them a serenade of welcome. While we are singing, the ushers pass cards to the visitors and we get their contact information. It is important to get this personal contact information through some process. The process must be immediate, dependable, consistent, and confidential. We then pass the "peace of Christ," which is an encouragement for worshipers to personally greet others near them with a handshake or "holy hug." The congregation looks forward to this special time of fellowship every week.

AUTHENTIC CHURCH GROWTH

Authentic church growth and genuine spiritual evangelism
result from a desire for communion with God and God's people.

1 Dynamic Holy Spirit communion in divine worship leads to a desire for spiritual fellowship with others and faith sharing.	2 Sharing faith and sincere invitations causes an invitee's spirit to perceive a salvific opportunity.
3 Invitee attends church and the church welcomes the Invitee, receiving him or her with love.	4 Invitee experiences dynamic communion of worship and the Invitee becomes a regular attendee and joins!

The critical phase of the CNE process comes after the worship where the visitor's contact information has been procured. How we treat visitors is important, but equally important is "what do we do once they are gone."[8] The next day, each visitor and every new member who joined are sent a correspondence to either thank them for visiting or to welcome them into our church family. This correspondence may be as simple as a postcard or as elaborate as a package of materials about the church. All of the visitors and new members to whom I have spoken appreciate this gesture of recognition and kindness.

Here is the pivotal point of the process: each visitor and new member receives a personal call from the pastor or the pastor's personal representative, echoing the church's joy in his or her attendance. Pastors must learn their members and the community or culture in which they live in order to effectively minister to them. The best way to find out the culture of a people is to talk with them and discover their spiritual backgrounds.[9] God has revealed to me that it is not how many members a church has but how well that church is ministering to their needs. Success is not being the largest church; it's being the largest church you can be.[10]

I am thankful to the officers and members of DuPage. They cherish their own personal experience of this initial pastoral contact so much that they allow me a decreased emphasis on business meetings, which are as time consuming and energy draining as they are important, so that I may call and supervise the calling of visitors and new members. Many persons exclaim to me that they have never had a pastor call them, and I believe that this small personal extension has greatly contributed to our church's evangelistic success. The primary spiritual reason that people join church is not because they are enthralled with our spiritual charisma or biblical knowledge. People join because they are in need of the loving care of God. The pastor and members are conduits for this care and "people don't care how much we know until they know how much we care."[11] As our church has grown, this area of evangelism has become an increasing challenge for me, but by God's grace, it is still a priority for our ministry.

Appropriating New Members

He destined us for adoption as his children through Jesus Christ, according to the good pleasure of his will.   — EPHESIANS 1:5

When persons join, they also receive correspondence and a telephone call encouraging them to attend the membership class. I teach this class each week. It is a wonderful opportunity not only to help new members become properly oriented to their new church home, but also for us as pastor and parishioner to become familiar with each other. Rick Warren says in his book *The Purpose-Driven Church*, "The most important class is the membership class and the senior pastor should teach some of it." This is important because new members are not only made to feel at home by becoming familiar with the history, theology, administration, and ministry opportunities of their

THE EVANGELISM PENTAGON

Steps of closed net evangelism.

Create a culture of church evangelism by:

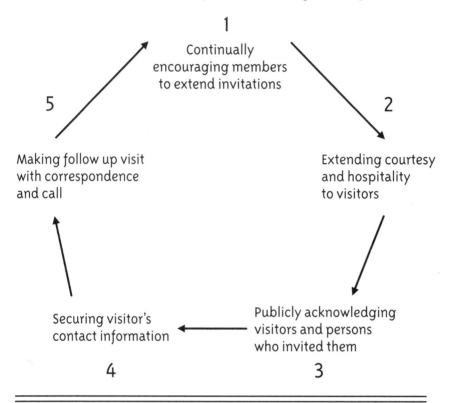

1
Continually
encouraging members
to extend invitations

5

2

Making follow up visit
with correspondence
and call

Extending courtesy
and hospitality
to visitors

Securing visitor's
contact information

Publicly acknowledging
visitors and persons
who invited them

4

3

new church, but because a sense of belonging is instilled when they are personally acquainted with their pastor. In this initial, formal introduction to the church, the "back door," or the potential that new members will slip away from the church once their initial fervor has diminished, is reduced. Consequently, the potential for them to become active, participating members who are likely to remain with the church increases. Assimilate new members intentionally because when new member assimilation is made a priority in a planned, deliberate fashion, the church is usually blessed with growth.[12]

SAMPLE VISITOR FOLLOW-UP CALL DIALOGUE

* Hello, my name is _____ , and I am calling on behalf of _____ Church. How are you this evening?

* On behalf of our pastor, _____ , I am simply calling to thank you for visiting with us this Sunday. I hope it was a blessing to you and that you enjoyed it.

* Are you familiar with our church at all? Do you have any questions about the church?

* Is there anything I can help you with while we are on the phone?

* If you have any questions please give me [optional] or the church office a call at _____ .

[Optional:] Ask them if they have any prayer concerns. Make sure you record them and communicate your prayers back to the pastor, minister, or outreach team.

* Thank you again for worshiping with us, and we certainly hope to see you again soon.

* Goodbye!

CNE is an effort of long-term commitment for the pastor and the faithful members who work its process, but it has been most gratifying. I am happy to say that I know almost every person of our two-thousand-member congregation by name and therefore am able to personally minister to them or refer them to the appropriate ministry when the need arises. I believe this starts with CNE. I don't apply any overt pressure on people to join the church or to become active in any particular ministry. I only thank God for the people God sends to worship with us and then exhort them to "let the Spirit lead!" All visitors don't join, and all members don't become active, but many of them do. Whether they join, become active, or not, I feel that I have done God and the people some service. I know that in

SAMPLE NEW MEMBER FOLLOW-UP CALL DIALOGUE

◆ Hello, my name is _____ and I am calling on behalf of _____ Church. How are you this evening?

◆ On behalf of our pastor, _____, I would like to welcome you to our church family, and we hope you are happy about your decision to join with us.

◆ You should receive a letter this week confirming the same and encouraging your attendance at the New Members Class, which meets at _____. _____ teaches the class, and it's a good time for you to meet [him or her] and for [him or her] to meet you.

◆ Are you familiar with our church at all? Do you have any questions about the church?

◆ Are there any questions I can answer while I have you on the phone?

◆ We hope to see you in the New Members Class. We thank God for your decision to join us and look forward to working with you in the Lord.

◆ If you have any questions please give me [optional] or the church office a call at _____.

[Optional:] Ask them if they have any prayer concerns. Make sure you record them and communicate your prayers back to the pastor, minister, or outreach team.

◆ Goodbye!

---

a larger congregation or one where other circumstances prevail, the CNE process may require some adjustment. In some cases the pastor can't personally call every visitor and new member. Every system has its challenges. Sometimes I have had church members who have a special gift in this area to assist me in calling. But it is commonly repeated in our meetings, whenever the topic arises, that there is a special blessing when the pastor calls. In addition, the reciprocal

CNE — CLOSED NET EVANGELISM

Evangelism Outreach to Persons
Already in Our Sphere of Influence

1. Always have church materials to share, preferably the Sunday Bulletin.

2. Share them with persons whom you encounter as you go about your normal activities.

3. Be hospitable to persons who visit your church.

4. Allow visitors to introduce themselves, document them and celebrate them.

5. Follow up their visit with a personal call, appreciative correspondence, and subsequent strategic mailings and/or encouragements, *but don't pressure them!*

---

spiritual growth and the ministerial fulfillment I gain through this personal pastoral outreach is an added dimension of blessing. It helps to keep me humble and to keep me from being "so heaven bound that I am no earthly good." Pastoral and parish ministry is basically a personal ministry of God for the parishioner. It is not so much a group dynamic or a mob action mentality because, ultimately, each person must stand individually before the throne of God at judgment. At DuPage, we are living witnesses that our faith in this area has born much fruit for Christ and his Realm.

We retain our visitor correspondence information for a designated time, sending visitors our church materials such as newsletters, program flyers, and ministry announcement cards. We are never pushy about imploring persons to join our church. We just continue for a while to kindly send information about God, the church, and the ministry. It takes the Holy Spirit longer to work on some persons than on others. In a steady fashion, God has always sent the increase. Church congregations may be likened to the buildings in which they worship. They are built "brick by brick" or "person by person." CNE helps us to effectively reach out to each individual household, become acquainted with them, and then celebrate them as precious treasures in the eyes of God. We have now expanded CNE to include follow-up calls to visitors and new members at intervals of one, three, and six months after their first visits or joining. This allows us to gauge whether or not they have found a church home or have gotten properly oriented to the DuPage family.

Finally, let me emphasize that regardless of what program or method is used in evangelistic efforts, or for any other efforts in Realm-building work, when there is success, it is not the program or method that has worked. It is God who has worked! "The method is never the key to accomplishing God's purposes. The key is your relationship with God."[13] "According to the grace of God given to me, like a skilled master builder I laid a foundation" (1 Cor. 3:10).

TWO

Administration

Now there are varieties of gifts, but the same Spirit; and there are varieties of services, but the same Lord; and there are varieties of activities, but it is the same God who activates all of them in everyone.

— 1 CORINTHIANS 12:4–6

Patience Is a Virtue

Wait for the Lord;
be strong, and let your heart take courage.

— PSALM 27:14A

As was stated in the preface, when I was appointed to the pastorate of DuPage, the church was already looking to purchase a new church building. We began working together as a church family, implementing and practicing the initiatives outlined in this book, and the need for a larger church facility dramatically increased. Even though, however, our bishop had directed me to "go and build a church," I had seen more than one building vision fail because the push and rush toward its implementation proved fatal.[1] Therefore, I did not come in and say, "We are going to build a church rather than buy one." This would have created another debate and possible schism in an already delicate situation. Instead, I joined with them in the pursuit of acquiring a church building. As God would have it, our efforts bore little fruit.

One church that we considered was priced far beyond even the flexible limits of our budget. I admit that I did not exercise much faith with this option because although it was a large and modern facility with offices, classrooms, and a gymnasium, the sanctuary seated only 200 worshipers. When we first arrived at DuPage, the congregation numbered approximately 150 members with an average of about 75 worshipers each Sunday. Approximately a year into our ministry together, the congregation had already grown to about 250 with an average of about 150 worshipers. We were holding two Sunday morning worship services in order to accommodate the growth. The church building considered was more of an administrative and activity facility than it was a worship facility. It was impressive but would not have accommodated the vision that God was manifesting for our ministry.

Our search led us to another church building that was also for sale. It was located in the downtown area of our suburb. It had a sanctuary large enough to accommodate our needs, but it did not have adequate parking. It was an older facility than the one previously mentioned and was in need of some repair and redecoration. We looked at several other buildings, and I am sorry to say that in one case we did not feel that we were dealt with fairly. We made several offers on the property but the price continued to rise with each offer. I pray now for those persons with whom we could not seem to find agreement.

Letting Go of the Old Building

But when Christ came as a high priest of the good things that have come, then through the greater and perfect tent (not made with hands, that is, not of this creation), he entered once for all into the Holy Place.
— HEBREWS 9:11

The congregation began to move its efforts in another direction. It began to think about expanding our current facility. Certain officers were the proponents of this idea. I was not in favor of this idea, but I kept my feelings to myself. Our church home was beautiful, quaint, and a historic old chapel of a church building. The members attached a great deal of sentiment to it. I think any pastor who has been in this situation knows exactly what I am talking about, and also knows what a huge obstacle this was. Many building projects have succumbed to the sentimental attachment that the congregation has for the old building. Many congregations have refused to be obedient to the vision God has for them simply because they did not want to move. And many congregations have diminished to a few families with a handful of members because of such unfaithfulness. If only we had the attachment to God that we have to our church buildings and the love of God that we have for the brick and mortar that surrounds us!

Our church building was a great blessing from the Lord that had fulfilled its purpose in its season, but its season had passed. It had been constructed seventy years earlier, in large part by the church members themselves. None of its carpentry, electrical, or plumbing infrastructure was up to code, and the suggested increase in seating capacity and overall square footage was still minimal. To expand that building would have been an insufficient panacea for our needs. Our growth potential would have been greatly limited by our desire for familiarity. Further, the church was located on a serene, tree-shaded avenue, which was a picturesque setting for a church. It, however, was hidden within a neighborhood that was difficult to access and was so hard to find that many visitors had to return twice in order to finally locate the church. The location of a church is an important factor in determining its growth.[2] While our location was a pleasant setting, it was not the best location for a church that wanted to grow.

Thankfully, in reviewing the plans that we submitted, the city required that by increasing our seating capacity we would have to supply commensurate off-street parking. This meant that we had to purchase many of the homes that were on the block. This was economically infeasible and upon inquiry we learned that those owners had no desire to sell their homes. Rev. Lana has a way of discerning the pivotal moments of life and ministry. On the day we received this news, I remember her saying, "This is our chance." Sure enough, the next time the trustee board met, the discussion turned from purchasing a church or renovating our current building to purchasing land in order to build a new church home. Hallelujah! I quickly authorized one of our trustees, a licensed real estate broker, to "go and find us some land." Now before we review some administrative initiatives that assisted us in facilitating this victory, let me first digress to lift up an important administrative point.

As you have read, there were two significant changes that the congregation made as we searched for a new church building. First, we moved through the activity of looking to purchase one. Then we moved through the idea of remodeling and expanding the old church building. The important point I wish to lift up is that as the pastor I had to wait on the Lord to direct the congregation. God's desire is for the pastor and the congregation to move forward together. "How very good and pleasant it is when kindred live together in unity!" (Ps. 133:1). It takes time to embed an idea in the life of a congregation, and although I planted many seeds of vision for a newly constructed church home, I did not force any action that might lead to congregational division in order to achieve the goal.[3] I worked with the officers and members even when the direction they were taking was not totally agreeable to me. I continually challenged my own personal spiritual growth so that my leadership was biblically based, divinely ordered, and not rooted in personal ambition or aspiration. Moses presents this model of representing God's authority by exemplifying his own subjection to it. "Now the man Moses was very humble, more so than anyone else on the face of the earth" (Num. 12:3). This affirms Ken Blanchard, John P. Carlos, and Alan Randolph's business assertion in their book *Empowerment Takes More Than a Minute:* "The traditional management model of the manager in control and employees under control is no longer effective."

Our Destination Was Divinely Located

Go forth from your country ... to the land that I will show you.
— GENESIS 12:1

Let me testify to the divine establishment of the location for our new church construction site. The first lot that we contracted to purchase was 1.5 acres on a busy road surrounded by office complexes. This may not seem to be a large parcel, but land is very expensive in our suburban community. I recently discovered that a fellow pastor in a suburb of another major city purchased thirty-two acres for the same amount we paid for this small parcel. To make this purchase was a great leap of faith for us at that time. Before we completed the purchase, however, another more appealing lot of 1.6 acres in a location near to this lot became available. Situated in a residential area opposite a public park, its asking price was 65 percent of the first lot's purchase price.

We would get more land in a more desirable location for nearly half the price! A euphemism that is purely African American comes to mind: "Ain't God good!" We paid a small fee to cancel our previous contract and purchased this graceful presentation at a savings of many thousands of dollars. Even so, we would not be able to begin construction for three years while we continued to grow, save money, and pay for the land. The systematic approach of our building program continued in a fashion called "phase building," or completing the construction project in stages. During the initial construction of the church, only the sanctuary and restrooms were completed. The following year we finished our fellowship hall and dining area. Next, we completed two expansions of our parking lot.

Finally, our balcony, classrooms, and all of the other areas were completed. Phase building allowed us to complete our facility in an economically advantageous fashion. We paid cash for all improvements subsequent to the first stage, thereby not incurring additional debt beyond the construction loan for the initial stage, which was the sanctuary. Currently, new land parcels have been acquired for future expansion and the vision continues as the Lord directs. But we are getting ahead of the story. This visible manifestation of blessed progress does not detail the administrative restraint, pastoral patience, inspired initiatives, and congregational cooperation that sustained us "through many dangers, toils, and snares." In the words of an old R&B tune, "Let's get down to the real nitty-gritty."

Change Requires Work

See, I am sending you out like sheep into the midst of wolves: so be wise as serpents and innocent as doves.   — MATTHEW 10:16

One evening several years into our ministry at DuPage, we were having a testimonial service. At that service, one of our church's founding members publicly testified that for a time after I was appointed as their pastor, there was much dissension over the direction our church began to take. His testimony revealed that, despite my best efforts to proceed in a non-confrontational manner, the congregation was struggling with spiritual, financial, and emotional challenges. The comfort of an unchanging worship schedule, the familiarity of routine activities, and the security of all of the members personally knowing each other was gone. The anxiety of this predicament found its expression in board meetings and church conferences. The ministerial staff differed in theological understanding. Board members wrestled with mixed feelings of loyalty to the former pastor or to me. The congregation was often frustrated with the continual adjustments we made to accommodate our growth. We often attempted to assuage our stress with assurances that growth was a good problem to have. But that recognition seldom was effective in reducing congregational stress. To the common reader with no exposure to such matters, this might seem like an overdramatization. But to anyone who has had some experience in this area, I'm sure that this scenario resonates in your spirit.

I adopted a posture of equity and fairness in decision making. Although there were several factions and small interest groups, I always tried to consider the best interests of the church and not show any group undue favoritism. In fairness, I tried to give everyone a little of what they wanted and a little of what they needed. This approach resonates with the Apostle Paul's confession in 1 Corinthians 9:22b, "I have become all things to all people that I might by all means save some."

This is an opportune juncture to insert the "practical theology" of church administration. Pastors and people must meet each other where they find each other. Through commitment and compromise they work together, so that God's will is done "on earth as it is in heaven" (Matt. 6:10b). I believe "spirituality must meet practicality." After all, God, who is Spirit, is also a practical God.[4] If we cannot accept this, then to some extent we deny the very advent of Christ. God appeared in human form and "...the Word became flesh and lived among us" (John 1:14a). Paul wrote of Christ to the Philippians in 2:7 that he was "born in human likeness. And...found in human form." By appearing in human form, God met humankind where we were. This was the most practical endeavor of Holy God, "who is Spirit" (John 4:24a).

This scriptural interpretation has undergirded my administrative philosophy. In sitting as chairperson of many meetings where sensitive issues were discussed, I walked the "middle line" of objectivity. I humorously referred to myself as being more of a referee than a chairperson. My job was to keep the officers from getting so mad at each other or at me that the vision would be defeated. In fact, my primary role was in being both the keeper of the vision and the keeper of the peace. Through experience I learned the techniques that helped us avoid many organizational pitfalls.

"First, I tell them I have something to tell them. Then, I come back later and tell them what it is."
— Morgan Freeman's character DCI William Cabot
from the movie *The Sum of All Fears*

Prepare the way . . .
— Mark 1:3b

One of the administrative techniques employed was the pastor's delegation of individuals and small committees to present ideas to the larger boards and church conferences. I call it "Ripple Effect Administration" (REA). I'm sure everyone has had the experience of throwing a stone into a pond and watching as it disturbed the water. The waves of the stone's disturbance emanate outward from its point of entry. The basic premise of REA is this: when a progressive idea is presented to a board or church conference, there is a natural inclination on the part of the people not to readily receive it. Many an idea of a pastor has succumbed to the lack of support when it was initially presented in a board meeting.

Many a congregation, when receiving a pastoral revelation, has listened intently to the revelation and then quickly sank it in the "sea of forgetfulness." It's true that people respond to vision, not need,[5] but more importantly, people must be prepared to understand vision.[6] REA is a process of broaching a new idea to a board or church conference in a way that makes the idea readily receivable. It begins by the pastor first relating the idea to one or two persons, and they

RIPPLE EFFECT ADMINISTRATION

together research the idea. The small group is a sort of informal committee. A presentation is then made by a designated member of the
small group to the appropriate church board. The significance of a
church member presenting the idea, and not the pastor, cannot be
diminished. Some church officers and board members have the idea
that their jobs are to protect the church from the pastor. This is especially true in cases where the pastor is newly appointed. Therefore,
an idea presented to the board by a member who is "one of them"
can be received more readily.

A primary importance for having committees is to provide boards
with intelligent information for their discussion.[7] The operative word
is "discussion." I would advise that new ideas are never initially presented for decision. Initially they should be presented for discussion.
This allows the seeds of divine revelation to gestate in the spirits of

the board members without the pressure of making a decision. Such pressure would surely lead to heated debate, followed by a tabling of the idea at best and a defeat, or even a board rebellion, at worst. Romans 8:25 says, "But if we hope for what we do not see, we wait for it in patience."

The board will invariably require more information. The committee can then be empowered to continue developing the proposal for presentation at the next meeting. This is the first step toward victory. The project is on the table! The committee can acquire the information and, more importantly, facilitate the board in taking ownership of the idea. When someone in the group, rather than you, promotes your goals, the ownership will be much greater.[8] The board's enthusiasm for the project will increase and the friendly relationships among the board members will fuel a positive wave of momentum. At subsequent board meetings, with some pastoral nudging, the idea has a high probability of receiving a favorable vote.

This process can then be repeated as the board presents the project to other administrative bodies in the church until it reaches the inevitable church conference meeting. The blessing of REA is that by the time it reaches the church conference, most of the people present will have already voted in favor of the project in the previous board meetings. The project is no longer new. It is a familiar, well-researched endeavor that the officers and members have helped develop. The congregation more readily accepts ideas fostered in this way. At the point of the ultimate and authorizing vote, the members vote positively for projects that are processed through the church in this manner. Such votes can even be quick and unanimous. The members are anxious to see the vision manifested in the anticipated project.

REA will serve any pastor or member in cultivating the seeds of revelation that God plants in each of us for his work. It must be adapted to varying institutional frameworks and administrative structures, but it can be applied generically for almost any effort. With REA, DuPage continues to make wonderful strides toward growth. During my tenure as pastor, we have purchased six residential homes for ministry purposes, and three land parcels, and the congregation has moved its worshiping location twice. We met in a Holiday Inn (we called it the "Holy Day Inn") for over two years as our church was being constructed. In these transitions, we have gone from one, to two, and now to three worship services. We have consummated three separate multi-million-dollar transactions. By the grace of God, we have not split as a congregation, have never experienced widespread dissension, and have continued to grow consistently. REA works, but in the rare cases where it cannot be applied, God will always provide other avenues for effecting ministry. "And there are varieties of service, but the same Lord" (1 Cor. 12:5).

Before moving on, let me honestly say that every initiative I promoted did not pass the boards. My preference was voted down a few times. It was at these times that I learned to wait on the Lord and pray. I earnestly sought assurance of the direction God would have me go. God always spoke to me. Either I was to present the initiative at a later time or I came to understand that the board's decision was more edifying for the ministry. Watchman Nee states, "Leaders should not make waves, but recognize the wave of God is spirit and ride it. Church leaders, both ministerial and lay, must beware of the fact that the difficulty today is that many of God's servants are either too bold or too strict or too overbearing."[9] These awkward situations gave me the opportunity to model support for an idea other than my own. I continue to tell my board members to "speak your mind and vote your conscience, but when we leave the meeting, we leave unanimously." I used my modeling of Christian character in these circumstances as teaching moments. This made a great and positive impression on my congregation.

At the other times, it was made plain to me that God wanted me to step out on faith and pursue an unpopular direction. Through prayer, the Holy Spirit emboldened my soul and comforted my spirit. God gave me the words to speak to the people and strengthened me until these prophetic messages were proven. In the process, I grew spiritually. "We know that all things work together for good for those who love God, to those who are called according to his purpose" (Rom. 8:28).

THREE

Stewardship

Bring the full tithe into the storehouse, so that there may be food in my house, and thus put me to the test, says the Lord of hosts; see if I will not open the windows of heaven for you and pour down for you an overflowing blessing. — MALACHI 3:10

Programs

...a time to break down, and a time to build up...
— ECCLESIASTES 3:3B

WHEN I ARRIVED AT DuPAGE, funds were being raised in a way that is traditional in many churches. DuPage was not a tithing church; it was a program church. By program church, I mean that it routinely raised the major portion of its funds through special programs and events outside of the Sunday morning offering. I'm sure that the congregation was aware of the biblical practice of tithing, which is the giving of the first 10 percent of a member's income for the support of the church. But they did not emphasize tithing as the primary means of financially supporting the church. There was no active program or process to intentionally teach and challenge the congregation in tithing.

Under the fiscal program in place, throughout the year various fund-raising programs were sponsored by different auxiliaries of the church. These programs supplemented the Sunday morning offerings. Such programs are a traditional way in which most African American churches have raised money for the ongoing expenses of the church. Programs are wonderful vehicles for fellowship. In small churches where the membership has modest incomes or in churches that once were large but now have diminished membership, this type of fiscal program may be necessary to adequately cover church expenses. Fund-raising programs can be the height of creative expression when a congregation is struggling to meet its obligations. I don't want to negate the importance of programs in raising funds for the church. Even the largest "mega congregations" have capital campaigns for their multi-million-dollar projects. These campaigns are no more than high ticket fund-raising programs to procure offerings above the tithe for specific purposes. Fund-raising programs are a regular source of receipts for religious institutions.

One reason programs are a necessary supplement to church receipts is the 20 percent reality. In the average congregation, 20 percent of the members do most of the work and give most of the money. When tithing is intentionally taught, however, and a deliberate process to practice tithing is established in the church, a greater percentage of the church membership will financially support the church. Programs then become opportunities for fellowship and spiritual growth, as opposed to fund-raisers. In order to accomplish this, a structured initiative of preaching, teaching, and practicing tithing must be presented to the congregation. As stated in George Barna's *The Habits of Highly Effective Churches,* "Highly effective churches never assume that they can simply expect people to give to the church" (148).

Take Deliberate and Measurable Steps of Faith

But to each one of us was grace given according to the measure of Christ's gift. — EPHESIANS 4:7

The first step in guiding DuPage toward becoming a tithing church was to learn about the existing programs and assess their fiscal effectiveness. I began to speak about increasing our giving on Sunday and decreasing our dependence on programs. I challenged the congregation to reduce the annual fund-raising programs to two annual days for fund-raising. These were Men's Day and Women's Day. All the other days, like Usher Day, Missionary Day, Church Anniversary Day, etc., would be special programs for acknowledgment and fellowship. There would be no financial obligation, such as fifty dollars per member, attached to these programs.

I asked them to add up all of the special offerings that they gave during the year for these programs. I offered them examples with the monetary calculations. They were to divide the total annual amount by fifty-two, and simply increase their regular offerings on Sunday by that amount. The members were challenged to make thoughtful determinations on how much their regular sacrificial offerings would be. As Paul directs in 1 Corinthians 16:2, "Set aside a sum for your offering." In short, they were instructed that we were moving toward becoming a tithing church by this small expression of faith without the immediate obligation of tithing.

This was a great step of faith because we were changing a proven process, hoping that there would be an increase in the total church offerings by the end of the year. Some members commented that the loss of the special program money would not be made up by the Sunday offerings. But I continuously articulated the direction God had given me and trusted the Lord for the increase. The members responded favorably, and that first year our receipts increased 76 percent over the previous year! The next year, we instituted the annual stewardship campaign, which is outlined later in this chapter. It continues to be the foundation of our fiscal program, and we continue to see an increase in our annual receipts.

Follow through with the Process

But be doers of the word, and not merely hearers who deceive themselves.
— JAMES 1:22

Our annual stewardship campaign is not anything novel or unique. It is simply a standardized, annual campaign to educate and motivate the congregation in stewardship and tithing. Its effectiveness is in the consistency with which it is fully implemented. It validates those who are already tithing and instructs those who are "growing in tithing." Every member should tithe or be growing in tithing. Growth in tithing is evidenced by increased offerings. From a spiritual perspective, the increased offerings are not relegated to the giving and receiving of mere money. Increased offerings are expressions of personal sacrifice and faith. It is faith that the Lord rewards,

TRANSFORMATION
FROM A PROGRAM SUPPORT CHURCH
TO A TITHING CHURCH

1. PROGRAM SUPPORT
Each auxiliary or member brings an extra offering for various events throughout the year.

2. STEWARDSHIP
Members are challenged to increase their weekly offerings by the total amount of all extra offerings divided by 52.

> Example:
>
> $100   Women's Day
> $50   Usher's Day
>   + $50   Missionary's Day
> $200   Extra Offerings
>
> $200 / 52 = $3.85
>   Increase offering each week

3. TITHING
Begin teaching stewardship and tithing.

---

and obedience that pleases God. This results in the abundant life that is promised throughout the scriptures to those who trust in God.

The primary component of the success of any program in the church is to implement and complete the steps of your plan. "The Christians in highly effective churches experience personal transformation because their church is committed to giving them systematic development experiences that have been carefully conceived, strategically implemented, and studiously evaluated."[1] As stated in C. Jeff Woods's *Better than Success: 8 Principles of Faithful Leadership*, "Most successful churches operate in accordance with a ministry plan. A ministry plan gives legs to the vision" (94–95).

The stewardship campaign consists of a few components that may be adjusted to better serve your specific congregation. First, the campaign takes an entire month, so a month of the year should be selected for the campaign. This month will be designated as Stewardship Month. Careful consideration should be given to the month's selection so that the campaign may have the optimal response from the congregation. I suggest the months of November or January, when the congregation is apt to be in full attendance. These are better than the summer months when members may be vacationing or other months when the Christian calendar is already full. The congregation should be made aware of the campaign before Stewardship Month so that they may prepare to prayerfully receive and consider the campaign materials. A congregational correspondence with introductory information should be sent to each congregant household the week before the first Sunday of Stewardship Month. Throughout the month, a weekly correspondence with information and materials should continue. The congregation must be continuously encouraged to prayerfully read the materials that they are receiving and to allow the Holy Spirit to lead them in their response. The first seed of the congregation's faith is to be attentive to the materials they are receiving.

Every Sunday a sermon on stewardship should be preached. The Sunday bulletin or worship guide should contain some information, directions, or statements on the subject of stewardship. The weekly Bible study of the church should focus on stewardship. The campaign should be infused with opportunities for tithers to give testimonies on the benefits of tithing.

The last Sunday in the campaign month is Commitment Sunday, when the church as a whole commits to becoming a tithing church. Posters, banners, and other displays throughout the church building can enhance the campaign. The campaign may be complemented by a workshop, a revival, or some other similar activity, where an outside person with some expertise in the area is brought in to teach or preach during the month. "Calling on outside experts, who are trained in specific areas, can be an excellent way to promote member development."[2] Such special events also provide an opportunity for

ANNUAL STEWARDSHIP CAMPAIGN

1. Select a month for the campaign.
2. Send weekly stewardship correspondence as well as motivational and informational materials.
3. Include stewardship information in bulletins each week.
4. Place posters throughout the church.
5. Teach a stewardship Bible Study series.
6. Preach each week on stewardship.
7. Have a Stewardship Commitment Day on the last Sunday of the month.
8. Use commitment cards and plan an extra event like a revival or workshop on stewardship during the month.

the officers and members of the church to take ownership of the campaign through the planning and leadership of such events. Including as many members as possible in the campaign's implementation will enhance the outcome of the campaign. Care must be taken in planning the campaign so that it is a comprehensive focus of the church body. Too many activities during Stewardship Month can diminish the campaign's impact. When the steps of this campaign are fully implemented, a noticeable increase in church receipts will occur.

Grow in Grace

My grace is sufficient for you.
— 2 CORINTHIANS 12:9

If the information on stewardship is properly tailored to your local congregation, it will result in an increase of faith and blessings for the church members, along with a significant increase in the church's monetary receipts. But there is a daunting reality about congregational stewardship. As we have seen, generally speaking, 20 percent of the church members give most of the church receipts. This imbalance of church support will continue to exist when there is no deliberate action to influence its correction. This imbalance also applies to the active servants and workers in the church. Only the intentional teaching of personal Christian stewardship can effect a correction of this imbalance. While continuing to preach, the teaching ministry must be invigorated to help increase the percentage of actual tithers.

There are certain aspects concerning the faith journey of the average member that are of importance to stewardship. The average member is preoccupied with the amount of money that tithing requires and not its scriptural imperatives or spiritual enhancements. The average member today sees tithing as a way to get blessings and not as a way to honor God. The church is called to facilitate the average member's spiritual growth and this includes the area of stewardship. The church must first assist the average member in personally accepting the spiritual priority of stewardship and then facilitate his or her interpretation of the scriptural imperatives. For this to occur, the church must do more than simply tell the member to tithe. It must offer practical processes for the member to appropriate tithing as a stewardship lifestyle.

This practical process can have the annual church stewardship campaign as its anchor. Throughout the year, a weekly reference to scripture with some instruction related to stewardship will provide members with the best opportunity for God to transform their life and for them to become good stewards. When the church's stewardship emphasis has the average member's spiritual growth as its standard for authenticity, increased financial receipts will result. As the church turns its priority from the need for more money to the spiritual growth of its members, the blessings of the Lord are evidenced not only in fiscal relief, but more importantly in the joy of the fellowship in the church. This joy becomes an attraction for more persons to join the church. It becomes an encouragement for more members to become good stewards. The faith journey of the entire congregation is encouraged.

Every person has a starting point where he or she chooses to be used by God. When a member has made the choice to be a tither, the

church must continually affirm that decision. If a member is praying about becoming a tither, the church must continually encourage
that member toward making that choice. I say "encourage" rather
than "challenge" because an encouragement is a challenge without
the liability of projecting guilt on the member. A feeling of guilt can
only motivate a temporary response from members and can cause
members to become dysfunctional in their ability to interact with
other members in a positive manner. Saturating a congregation with
a sense of guilt does not encourage a spirit of liberty in the congregation. "Where the Spirit of the Lord is, there is liberty" (2 Cor. 3:17).
Authentic spiritual growth will occur as God speaks to the heart of
the members. The response that individuals give to God will endure
beyond any response cajoled from them by pressuring them to tithe
from a feeling of guilt.

Tithing is God's way for people to support Christ's Realm. It is fair
in that 10 percent is the same amount for everyone, no matter what
their income is. Tithing is also a dependable way for the church's
ministries to be supported. It allows for a regular, consistent flow
of resources that the church can count on for its work. Tithing is a
discipline of sacrifice and reward. For those who practice tithing, it
is a certain avenue to discipleship that enlivens our faith. Stewardship is the Christian management of all that we are and all that we
have. It encompasses a discipline of responsibility and accountability. Through the devotion of our time, talents, and tithes, the Realm
of Christ increases.

My father often used colloquial expressions to give sound advice.
His favorite challenge to good stewardship was this blunt statement:
"Don't let old age and poverty meet you on the same corner." The
Bible promises a personal benefit of Christian stewardship. In Psalm
37:25, David asserts, "I have been young, and now am old, yet I
have not seen the righteous forsaken or their children begging for
bread." In connecting stewardship to spiritual maturity, however, a
qualification must contextualize any promise of blessing and reward.
Christian servants should tithe and contribute their services to the
church simply to be obedient to God. True obedience is fostered only
when the servant has an intimate and active relationship with God.

An intimate relationship with God is sustained through the disciplined practice of personal devotions, such as daily prayer, daily Bible study, regular worship, outreach work (e.g., missions, evangelism, etc.), periodic fasting, and tithing.

Through personal devotions, Christian servants understand that God truly does reward faith, but that the purpose of their faith is not to get blessings. The purpose of faith is to please God and build God's Realm. God's servants endure many "crucifixions" in their Christian service. Only the strength provided by a close personal relationship with God will sustain us to continue in faith and attain to God's "resurrections." Remember, outward appearances of success do not always indicate faith, and outward appearances of failure do not always indicate the lack of faith. Henry Blackaby states in *Experiencing God,* "Faithful servants are ones that do whatever the master tells them, in spite of the outcome." It is this sacrificial posture of the Christian servant that affords an undeniable access to God's transforming power.

Through developing a congregational sense of a spiritual perspective, the church moves closer to being a transforming agent of members and their communities. This is the victory of God in Christ Jesus that delivers us from the adversary of our spiritual warfare. Obedient and faithful stewardship establishes a firm foundation for this victory because it is our acknowledgment of the divine authority of Christ. As Watchman Nee says in *Spiritual Authority,* "Satan is not afraid of our preaching the Word of Christ, yet how very much he is in fear of our being subject to the authority of Christ."

God Honors Faith and Rewards Obedience

Indeed, by faith our ancestors received approval.
— HEBREWS 11:2

When I am blessed with an invitation to present a workshop on stewardship, most of the presentation covers the priority of developing and sustaining an active, personal relationship with God. A lesser portion of time specifically addresses tithing. No presentation on stewardship, however, would be complete without some reference to the pleasure God receives from persons who are willing to live out their faith. I generally conclude with a brief but dynamic affirmation of God's sure reward and blessings. I usually save the emphasis on blessings and rewards until the end because you cannot authentically serve God simply because of what you will receive for your service. It is our love for God that should be the reason for our service, not compensation. To emphasize blessings received from God over love for God is not only a travesty of faith, it is a perversion of the scriptures and a manipulation of God's people. We are called to serve God out of love and obedience for God, because God asks this of us (1 Sam. 15:22; Luke 6:46; John 14:15).

But it would also be incorrect to say that blessings from God do not result from the exercise of faith and obedience. The scriptures clearly reiterate that blessings and rewards result from faithfully serving God (Mal. 3:10; Matt. 6:31–33; Luke 6:38). Often the blessings will return in ways other than the service or sacrifice that was rendered. Sometimes the deliverance or the answer to prayer will not come right away, but it surely will come if you wait on God. Many times the reward of faith is a reconciliation of a personal nature that is a priceless treasure money cannot buy. Be encouraged and remain steadfast; the victory is surely on the way. Hallelujah!

Now that we have established stewardship and tithing as the primary source for church support, let us prepare to address the goal of the church's fiscal program. The spiritual goal of the church's fiscal program is to offer an opportunity for the faithful to exercise their faith, please God, and receive divine encouragement for their faith through reward and blessing. The practical goal of the church's fiscal program is to meet the church budget. In addressing the church's budget, I must first stress the point that the church finances and the church budget are two different things. The church finances are the fiscal receipts and expenditures of the church.

The church budget is the church's projection of receipts and expenditures. The budget is merely an outline of what the church thinks its finances will be. The point I am making is that neither the church finances nor the church budget are self-determining or interdependent. The finances do not depend on the budget and neither does the budget depend on the finances. They both depend on and are determined by the church calendar. The budget is only ink on paper. It is only an outlined projection of the anticipated finances that will be managed to support the church ministry. It is the calendar of programs, activities, and ministries that call the members to action, resulting in the church receiving something to manage. The programs, activities, and ministries are what involve the people, both spiritually and bodily, in the actual work of Realm building. When these involvements are deliberately scheduled throughout the year to optimize the support of the membership, then the life of the church will be more cooperative, complementary, vibrant, and productive. The church calendar, second only to the spiritual maturity of the membership, determines the fiscal potential of the church.

I once asked a fellow pastor how his ministry was progressing and what he was anticipating for Sunday worship. His response was "I have to wait and see who comes." Well, let me say this: if you are a pastor or church leader and you have to wait and see who comes to participate in and support your ministry, then you are never going to see much. I prayerfully work every week in faith with the thought of getting people to come to church so that they might grow in Christ and the joy of their salvation.

Every week, I ask myself, "What can we do this week to get the people to come to church?" Unless there is an implemented plan of ministry (i.e., something special that will cause the people to want to come to church), I cannot rest. I submit that whether it is a planned day of special celebration, a guest speaker, the choir, the children, or some outreach of spiritual purpose, there must be something every week that shouts to the congregation and the community, "The Lord is doing something special this week! Come and see what it is!" Chapter 4 will present how the church's calendar of programs and activities forms the basis of optimizing both the fiscal and human resources of the congregation.

FOUR

Raising the Church Budget

Set the Order of Things

For everything there is a season, and a time for every matter under heaven. — ECCLESIASTES 3:1

I N THE PREVIOUS CHAPTER, I established that stewardship in general, and tithing specifically, is the primary biblical source of fiscal support for the church. Let me reiterate that good stewardship, as evidenced in tithing, provides not only a solid fiscal foundation for the church, but more importantly, it promotes a scriptural integrity for the congregation that lends itself to continued and authentic spiritual growth. In order to facilitate a tithing mentality to support the work of the church, a practical program for stewardship was detailed. When this stewardship program is appropriated into the church's overall program, it will increase the potential for optimizing church resources and result in more faith and finances.

Now we will look at the activities of the church's various ministry programs with the purpose of planning a *fiscally effective* annual schedule. By fiscally effective I mean a schedule that is fiscally based on tithing and that is deliberately planned to optimize the church's human and fiscal resources throughout the entire year. If you don't get anything else from this chapter, and I certainly hope that you do, be sure to remember this one important fact: the calendar schedule of church programs and ministries is equally as important in raising the church budget as the programs and ministries themselves. "Significant impact depends on strategic approach."[1]

It is important to plan strategically in order to keep a positive spirit that will fuel the ongoing support of the church ministries in all of their various areas. Rick Warren says in *The Purpose-Driven*

Church, "Since no single ministry can accomplish all the church is called to do, we must depend on and cooperate with each other." When programs are not planned so that they are cooperative and complementary, there are conflicts in the use of church facilities and membership personnel that create unnecessary confusion and waste valuable energy. Also, when scheduling is not done with the idea of allowing certain resources, especially human and financial resources, to replenish themselves, then the church does not get the optimal response from its members. "The lifestyle of most people today reduces their time for volunteer work."[2] I believe that church members do their best to support the church, but if the timing of programs is more intentionally and considerately planned, they can better support them.

Plan for the Entire Year

So teach us to count our days.
— PSALM 90:12

As we look at the twelve months of the annual calendar, we immediately recognize that there are months and seasons of high and low activity in the church year. Before we begin scheduling, we must be prayerful about when the congregation is in its high and low response times. For instance, at DuPage the summer months are traditionally when most of the members travel for vacation; there are a lot of young parents and that is when the kids are out of school. We schedule some programs for the summer because Realm building work is continuous, but when we want the optimal response of church-wide participation, we don't schedule that program in the summer. It is the church members who support the church program and "a market driven church is people centered and not program centered."[3] In *Twelve Dynamic Shifts for Transforming Your Church*, E. Stanley Ott gives a concise and beneficial scriptural observation on this point, stating, "Jesus never began with programs; he began with people." Determining when your church has high and low seasons of congregational availability to support programs will be the first important observation you make when setting your calendar. You want to be realistic and plan for the best results. In addition, you must be as specific as possible in the selection of your program season, program month, and even the particular Sunday of the month, in order to ensure the best results for your effort.

After you have determined when to have your biggest programs, then you want to look at the activities of the church and determine what the "biggest" days of the year are. By big days I mean days of special celebratory worship services, significant spiritual impact, the largest church participation, generous offerings, or any combination of these. At DuPage, our big days are regularly scheduled on our annual calendar of church activities. We have at least one big day every month and most of our big days are for fellowship and not for fund-raising. They are primarily annual days of recognition for specific auxiliaries or outreach efforts of the church. For fiscal purposes, big days are days where the largest percentage of the congregation is called to lend specific financial support or offerings above the tithe.

Our fiscal big days of the year are Men's Day, Women's Day and Church Anniversary Day. I like to separate Men's and Women's Days not only so each group can have its time to address gender-specific issues and celebrations, but also because it gives the households time to recover financially and lend their best support individually to each day. In other words, in the households where there is a husband and wife, the money for church support is usually coming from the same budget. Separating the days gives that household the best chance to fully support the annual day effort.

And so, as we look at the annual church calendar, we are determining the times for optimal congregational support and deliberately positioning the biggest programs and the annual events that enlist the largest portions of the congregation in order to gain the best response and support for the programs. I challenge myself to always know and being able to share what is occurring on any given Sunday of the year. The church calendar is the backbone of raising the church budget.

Every pastor should approach this area of concern with the highest degree of responsible stewardship, and this stewardship should be reflected in his or her conscious knowledge of what is planned for each Sunday of the year. I cannot express the direct and indirect benefits of this one point enough. God can really provide revelations to you about Realm building work when there is an open and active mental file on the work. The proper spacing of the biggest programs on the calendar allows for them to be individually planned, distinctly promoted, and optimally supported. A further goal in creating an increasingly effective church calendar is to pick or create three or four major events for the year. As previously mentioned, our major days, which are our fiscal big days, are Men's, Women's, and Church Anniversary Days. Ideally, each event should be spaced approximately three months apart on the calendar. In this way the congregation can be focused as much as possible on making each event a success.

Expand the Circle of Leadership

So I took the leaders of your tribes, wise and reputable individuals, and installed them as leaders over you.   — DEUTERONOMY 1:15A

Any good program for a church activity or ministry begins with a vision. Ideally, that vision is given from the Lord to the pastor or to a member who shares it with the pastor and the pastor approves it. Authentic divine vision is not faddish or self-elevating. "Faithful leaders commit to a vision because it comes from God, not because it is flashy."[4] The vision, which becomes an idea of something for the church to do, is a revelation and divine insight about the life and needs of the congregation. The idea coalesces into a program or activity that will address the need and enhance the life of the congregation. Once this has taken place, accountable leadership must be designated to be responsible for forwarding the idea, organizing the program, and implementing the plans for the event. I recommend that a member of the church should volunteer, be elected, or be selected for the leadership. Donald P. Smith says in *Empowering Ministry: Ways to Grow in Effectiveness*, "Never begin a new program without a layperson who is passionately caring for that program."

The pastor, who participates in the general oversight, should not have to worry about the details of the program. When members are placed in leadership roles, it not only allows them to take responsibility for making an event happen, but it also gives them the opportunity

SAMPLE CHURCH CALENDAR PLAN OF EVENTS

Month	First Set the Biggest Events	Then Set the Annual Events
January		Stewardship Day
February	Family & Friends Day	Founder's Day / Scouts Day
March	Men's Day	
April		Missionary Day / Young People's Department Day
May		Class Leaders Day
June	Women's Day	Church School Promotion Day
July		Visitors Day
August		Lay Day
September	Church Anniversary	Pastor's Appreciation
October		Community Service Day / Relationship Day
November		Usher Day
December		Officer Installation

Please note: Activities such as revivals, choir concerts, workshops, or other off Sunday events are not indicated.

These Sunday-planned annual events should not include special days such as Easter, Mother's Day, etc., unless special emphasis and committee organization efforts for activities and/or recognitions occur. This chart is only an example of Sunday planning.

to make a meaningful contribution to the church ministry. In this way they take ownership of the program and thereby inspire the church body to join in the effort. This becomes a comprehensive unification process for the entire church, which often complements the pastoral leadership. A fundamental way to have more participation and support for a program is to expand the opportunities of leadership for the program. This not only gets more people involved; it affords them an opportunity to grow spiritually through the exercise of their own spiritual gifts under the guidance of the pastor. "The responsibility of leadership is to constantly open up new areas of ministry in which people can utilize their gifts."[5]

The chairperson should select a committee who can then take responsibility for the various major areas of the effort, such as the reception, the program participants, announcements, correspondence and calling, the budget, and so on. "There must be systems in place to support the vision."[6] With this team in place, the chairperson also now allows others to participate in leadership roles. The chairperson is then free to act as an overall coordinator of the event, who communicates with the pastor. The more persons who are involved in the leadership, the more persons who will participate in the effort, and the greater the success of the event.

Of course, the number of leaders has to be manageable and, more than anything, they must understand the basic concept of spiritual authority. They must know that they are leaders who are also following and that "to obey is better than to sacrifice" (1 Sam. 15:22). Every person should be encouraged in their ideas, suggestions, and recommendations, but every person must be willing to support the decisions of their pastor and event chairperson. The Christian servant is always content in the liberty of being positioned simply to offer what he or she has for consideration.

There are entire books that expound on authority, obedience, and team cooperation. Obedience is the most basic spiritual axiom. Let it suffice to say that for an enjoyable, harmonious, and successful effort, this foundational directive is crucial and must be taught with consistency. As Rick Warren says in *The Purpose-Driven Church*, "How to implement ideas is as important as the idea itself." One of the most important ways of implementing ideas in a church program is to prayerfully present the idea at the beginning of the church year so that it may be included in the overall schedule of the church's activities. This assures that each effort will proceed in a complementary fashion. It is important to emphasize the pre-planning and scheduling of major events because their success depends greatly upon it.

The pastor must be considered the primary leader because the pastor has an insight on the congregation that few members have. There are a lot of personal histories and peculiar facts about the church family as a whole and the particular members who will be doing the work. The church family, and the members who make it up, are joined with God's plan for the purpose of their collective and individual faith journeys as saved children of God. Only the pastor has the full responsibility and accountability to God for the souls residing in the congregation. Leaders selected to carry out the programs must work in concert with the pastor's wisdom. "The pastor is the only one with the total overview of the congregation."[7]

Marketing and Promotion

David organized them according to the appointed duties in their service.
— 1 CHRONICLES 24:3B

A primary component of the organization and planning phase of an event should be the marketing and promotion of the program. Too many times we invest all of our energy in putting together an excellent program, only to be disappointed at the low number of persons who show up. One of the most disastrous assumptions about church programming is that the people are going to show up just because there is an event planned. There is an understanding about the church pertinent to this subject that can pay dividends in many areas of church life. That understanding is that the church is made up of faithful members who have made a commitment to the ministry, but they are still volunteers. Members are not paid to be there. They are there because they want to be there. There are a lot of other places that they could be. There are also a lot of other churches that they would attend. They don't have to be at your church. Members also have their own lives to live. Whether a pastor or church leader wants to accept it or not, this is a fact. Members have jobs, families, and other personal involvements and responsibilities. If the event being planned is to have the best opportunity for success, then its promotion must be a fundamental aspect of its planning.

Members and other potential attendees and supporters must be encouraged in their support. In doing this, a careful balance between promoting the program and applying too much pressure must be kept. Members should be encouraged to support the program and yet not be discouraged by extreme or obnoxious overtures. Too much pressure to attend a program or to become involved in one can be a turnoff to members. Placing a guilt trip on persons to gain their support can contradict positive spiritual energy surrounding the event and be self-defeating in terms of the member spiritual's growth. Nonetheless, an intentional and earnest effort, with as comprehensive an outreach as feasibly possible, must be undertaken to get as many people as possible to be "in the number" on the day of the event. The more work that is put into this outreach, the better the chances for a successful event. As my father was fond of saying about church events and programs, "If you don't push it, it won't go."

Promotional Techniques

Make known his deeds among the peoples.
— 1 CHRONICLES 16:8B

There are many ways to promote a program in a church. Traditional ways include Sunday morning announcements, bulletin inserts, newspaper advertisements, letters, flyers, phone calls. In *Marketing the Church,* George Barna says, "Marketing cannot occur without clear and meaningful communication." In order for marketing to be meaningful and have the maximum effect, it must be planned. And in order for the plan to realize its fullest potential, it should have a timeline of intermittent goals and move progressively through its timeline. With a timeline, each step can be fully attended to. Each step can be followed up as the plan moves forward so that the plan is fully implemented through each individual step. Follow-up increases quality.[8] This highlights the importance of a good chairperson. "While the pastors are focused on the big picture, they need people they can depend on to keep an eye on the details."[9]

With the major church events in place, the remainder of the church calendar can be scheduled. In completing a church calendar that will encourage member participation, provide optimum financial support, and generate positive spiritual energy, there should be one big program per month. Orbiting around the biggest days, which are the three or four major events of the church, should be monthly celebrations of some auxiliary or ministry of the church. These celebrations and special days are more for fellowship than for fund-raising. This keeps dynamic activity continuously generated in the church. It allows affirmation for the ministries and service areas of the church. It gives Sunday worship a change from its regular routine (see chapter 7).

Few people attend a particular church these days because they have some unbreakable tie to that church. People today attend a particular church primarily because there is something going on there that is appealing to them. Having a schedule of Sunday worship that highlights the life and work of the church is appealing to church members and attractive to visitors. Worship becomes dynamic and encourages excitement when its regular routine and order are adjusted for special events. There are many group celebrations and activities that can take their respective places in the church's programming schedule, such as Missionary Day, Usher Day, Stewardship Commitment Day, Lay Day, Annual Young People's Day, Pastor's Appreciation Day, Officers' Installation Day, and many others depending on the church's history and the ministries that are present in the church. The importance of the development and support of youth ministries cannot be overstated because "churches with growing attendance are always distinguished by flourishing youth ministries."[10]

Recognize and Utilize the Pastor

...and not only that, but he has also been appointed by the churches to travel with us while we are administering this generous undertaking for the glory of the Lord himself and to show our goodwill.

— 2 CORINTHIANS 8:19

The pulpit of the church and the worship that is led from it are the pastor's responsibility. The time for spiritual unction in a church is during its worship services. Only the servant whom God has set apart as pastor is authorized to reveal the direction that God has given for the congregation during the formal worship. "I will give you shepherds after my own heart, who will feed you with knowledge and understanding" (Jer. 3:15). The pastor directs the service. This basic fact of church leadership is mentioned to reiterate a qualification for implementing these special day programs.

All programs and their participants should be approved by the pastor before they are shared with the groups or put into action. Many times group leaders will initiate actions and conversations about setting a Sunday order of worship and selecting participants before it has been approved by the pastor. This can be an innocent oversight at best, but at its worst it can be no less than usurping pastoral authority. No member can take spiritual responsibility for a congregation and therefore no member should get ahead of the pastor in terms of determining the worship experience. In addition, when persons are invited to participate in church activities before the pastor gives approval, and the pastor subsequently disapproves, then embarrassment can occur when persons are notified of the change in the previously unapproved arrangements. This confusion is unnecessary but illustrates the importance of organization and communication before implementation.

Remember, the church is a volunteer organization in which persons have a strong emotional and spiritual investment. In order for the church to have success and for God to get the victory, there are many spiritual, personal, and procedural complexities that must be continually taken into consideration. Programs must be scheduled, planned, and implemented in a fashion that is appropriate for the church as a whole, the particular groups of recognition, and the specific individuals who are participating in order for things to be done "decently and in order" (1 Cor. 14:40). People must be cooperative in their participation but they should also be shown consideration by the special day leadership during the planning process, in order for "all things to work together for good" (Rom. 8:28b).

Working in the church provides the unique opportunity of accessing the power that comes from God. My mother loved to talk about "Holy Ghost Power." This is the real key for all church activities that transforms the worldly to the divine plateau of victory. Spiritual victory for the church is more than the number of persons in attendance or the amount of money that is raised. Spiritual victory is about improving the quality of life for people as they grow to become more like Christ. As Henry Blackaby says in his seminal work *Experiencing God: Knowing and Doing the Will of God*, "Although organizations and programs are designed to promote outreach growth and ministry, they can lead to shallow relationships and independence. If a church is not careful, it may be helping people experience a program and miss a personal encounter with the loving Christ." Spiritual power that comes from God can be accessed only by the methods God has laid out in the Holy Scriptures. The common denominator of these methods, especially when serving in the church, is humility and obedience. The church is uniquely positioned to teach this basic lesson to God's people. "The church is the place where obedience can be learned since there is not really such a thing as obedience in this world."[11]

Every Sunday Is Special

This is the day that the Lord has made; let us rejoice and be glad in it.
— PSALM 118:24

Once the annual calendar of the church has been set, the monthly schedule of activities and Sunday morning worships can be filled in. I always ask myself, apart from the obvious, what reason does the congregation have to come to church this Sunday? Remember, we are speaking of intentionally programming the church so that the optimum fiscal support and member participation can result. Theoretically, every Sunday can offer something special to inspire the membership and motivate them to invite guests to worship. Some regular monthly service events are Holy Communion Sunday, Baptism Sunday, Monthly Youth Sunday, New Members' Fellowship Sunday, Visitors Sunday. I'm sure you can think of others. When a Sunday service offers something special other than the regular order of worship, the anticipation can open a spiritual window for divine intervention. Miracles begin to occur because the strongholds of routine and rigidity are pulled down. Church becomes an exciting experience where something new is always happening, while at the same time, because of organization and planning, everything is done "decently and in order" (1 Cor. 14:40).

As the church calendar begins to fill, you may notice that there is more than one annual day event in a month. When one auxiliary has a recognition day, others may desire to have a day. This is where management and administrative expertise must come into play. Too many annual days will diminish the dynamic impact of the annual calendar schedule. This can also create confusion in the congregation's expectations of worship, which will destabilize the congregation. A major reason that people attend church is because it represents their faith in a secure and stable God. Therefore, in order to develop a dynamic but practical program, the pastor and the church leadership must set priorities regarding the schedule. The priority for approving special days for Sunday worship can be determined by asking several questions.

- Does the special day encourage participation by the entire church membership?

- Does it encompass and encourage participation by a major segment of the congregation?

- Does it recognize an auxiliary or ministry that is basic and primary to the mission of the church?

- Does it highlight a ministry or an outreach effort that is a key component of the church?

- How many members are active in the auxiliary?

- Is the special day significant to the history and foundation of the church?

- Does it have a specific Realm building purpose?

There are many factors to consider when setting an annual special day. Some events are best scheduled for times other than Sunday morning. There should be, however, at least one major program every month to optimize the resources of the church and to encourage a dynamic atmosphere in the church. If the calendar fills up and the month has more than one special day, the solution for getting the best effort and energy from the church rests on the sponsoring auxiliary or ministry group. The public platform for encouraging congregation-wide support must be reserved for the three or four major annual events. One of the purposes of planned scheduling is to avoid instances where two or more chairpersons are simultaneously competing for congregational support.

The group that is having a special day, which may be their annual day but is not one of the church's major days, must first be responsible for planning, organizing, and implementing efforts to maximize the involvement of their group. They should be active agents sponsoring the day's activities for the entire church rather than recruiters trying to get the whole church involved in their implementation efforts. This allows for activities to be scheduled on more than one day in the month while still having the best support from the church for the day.

There are two things about special days that are important to address at this point. One is the special day Sunday order of worship, or the program itself, and the other is the financial aspect of special days in general. For the Sunday order of worship, the time frame is very important. It is still Sunday worship and people primarily come to church on Sunday to worship God, not to attend a program. If the program is to include a multitude of recognitions, acknowledgments, and award presentations that cannot be done expeditiously, then that program may be better suited for a time other than Sunday morning. The church calendar should have a regular progression of special days and events to diversify the Sunday morning worship experience and add to its dynamism. Auxiliaries and ministries, however, cannot be allowed to usurp the Sunday morning worship with the social, political, and recreational aspects or their organization. A special day must be planned with a goal of balancing the spiritual worship with the practical recognition of the occasion. It must recognize and highlight a ministry, but not unduly prolong the worship or diminish its spiritual potential of praise.

As for the financial aspect of special days, there should be no more than three special days that have a special offering or pledge attached to them. The other special days should be for fellowship and not for the auxiliary or church members to make a special pledge or offering for that day. The members of the church should generally support the church through tithes and regular offerings, such as missionary offering, church school offering, building fund offering, etc. In order to get the maximum fiscal support of the church from the membership, the membership must be intentionally educated and continuously encouraged in tithing (see chapter 3). Otherwise, instead of the members regularly bringing their sacrificial tithes and offerings to the church in a disciplined and dependable manner, the congregation will constantly be begged for money. This wears down the desire of the congregation to support the ministry and ultimately is counterproductive to their spiritual development and fiscal support.

Revelation Resides in the Obvious

The wisdom of this world is foolishness with God.
— 1 CORINTHIANS 3:19

Offering the church membership a schedule of special-day worships is not a novel concept. Special days have been a regular part of church life for a long time. As Jim Collins, however, says in *Good to Great*, "The essence of profound insight is simplicity." What I am emphasizing is the significant fiscal impact and the noticeable increase in member participation that a well organized and implemented calendar of special days can have. When the success of the ongoing activities of the church is taken for granted, then they are not enthusiastically promoted or anticipated with a high degree of excitement. The result is a loss of resources that are greatly needed to further the mission of Christ. "A strategy for continuing success has to be applied on an ongoing basis."[12] An effective church program must have a church calendar of special days and activities that is deliberately structured and managed so that congregational support can reach its highest potential.

Additionally, "no program is meant to last forever."[13] Once you have determined a calendar of set programs and special days, as time goes on you will discover that some events will lose their significance and their ability for positive impact on the life and mission of the church. There may be various reasons for this, such as the sponsoring auxiliary diminishes in its service capacity, the neighborhood demographics shift, cultural changes create different needs, new creativity is needed to spark the congregation's interest, etc.

Thomas Ettinger and Helen R. Neinast say in *The Long and Winding Road*, "Rituals are repeated patterns of meaningful acts." Church programs are meaningful acts but they are not sacraments. A ritual is any routine of activity that we regularly perform. Under this definition, the way we brush our teeth, shower, and dress is our morning ritual. The point is that when an activity, specifically a special day program, ceases to provide meaning and fulfill the purpose of its original intent, then that is a ritual or regular activity of the church that must be re-evaluated. "Change is constant," Disraeli said. The vibrancy of the church ministry depends upon its continued relevance to both contemporary society and the current need of its parishioners. In order to be effective in serving the present age, "new traditions can be developed and integrated into the church."[14]

Finally, the spiritual context of our programming must always be emphasized. We can spend so much time strategizing, organizing, and planning that we forget that the church is God's spiritual creation on earth. In terms of techniques or methods, we must remember, "It never works. God works!" Almighty God and our relationship to God are the primary determinants for the success or failure of anything that we propose or endeavor in God's name. In the end, all that matters is that God is glorified, the gospel of Jesus Christ is proclaimed and the people of God once more have God's glory revealed to them.

FIVE

Planning Capital Projects

If you are a numerous people, go up to the forest, and clear ground there for yourselves.... — JOSHUA 17:15A

WHEN BISHOP MAYO appointed me as the pastor of DuPage with the words, "Go, and build a church," he was directing me into a capital construction project. A capital construction project may be defined as any construction project that requires financial and human resources beyond the means of the church's normal operation. For us to envision a multimillion-dollar building program with only two hundred members on a $100,000 budget was certainly an endeavor beyond the means of the church's normal operation. As the new and first full-time pastor of DuPage, I had to learn who my members were and how we might work together.

Our first challenge together was to realize and accept the need for a building program. As Barna states in *Marketing the Church*, "The first test of a director is to develop an ownership of the plan (vision) in the church members." As a new pastor, I could not effectively lead the people in a direction that they didn't want to go. No one would accept or support the great challenge of a building program without first understanding that a need did exist.

An Objective Facility Assessment

I went out by night by the Valley Gate past the Dragon's Springs and to the Dung Gate, and I inspected the walls of Jerusalem that had been broken down and its gates that had been destroyed by fire.

— NEHEMIAH 2:13

The church building that we occupied was a wonderful cinder block, gable-roof chapel like many you see in rural settings. Painted white and sitting on a quiet, secluded street, it represented a peaceful place of refuge from the hectic pace of society. There were, however, many problems with the building. It was old and its electrical and plumbing infrastructure was outdated and required constant maintenance. The seating capacity in the sanctuary was inadequate. We were holding two services on Sunday and, before we moved out, we began a third service on Saturday night. There wasn't enough space for board or auxiliary meetings even after we acquired the house next door and renovated it. The building facilities did not have the conveniences and accommodations necessary to house a growing ministry.

Even though, however, a church building may be inadequate for the congregation's activities, a congregation develops a great emotional attachment to both its building and the neighborhood. DuPage was no exception. Because of this emotional attachment, the shortcomings of the building were overlooked by most of the congregation. As the problem of inadequate facilities persisted, the congregation acquiesced to the increasingly evident need for a larger and more modern building. This is what led them to begin shopping for a new church by looking at the already constructed churches that were available in the community. They were involved in this process when I was initially appointed.

There were several churches on the market in our general vicinity at that time. Most of the available church buildings were either too old or had inadequate parking, or there were other characteristics about them that were not consistent with the progressive change we needed. We narrowed our selection to two churches, selected the one we felt would best suit our needs, and made an aggressive attempt to purchase it. This was our most promising scenario, but negotiations broke down because of an inability to come to an agreement with the sellers on the price. In pursuing our second option, we made offers on the property that were verbally accepted by the sellers, but subsequent to their verbal agreements, the sellers made repeated requests for a higher purchase price. We agreed to their first few requests for a higher purchase amount, but as those requests continued, we decided not to continue those negotiations.

We made one more attempt at purchasing another facility, but by then emotions about leaving the old church home began to surface.

When our effort to purchase that church failed, the congregation's sentiment shifted from purchasing a church to renovating and expanding the old church building. I was not in favor of this idea, but its occurrence was not unexpected. "At some point people don't resist new ideas, they resist change."[1] We had some initial sketches drawn to show what our expanded church would look like, detailing all of the improvements and accommodations it would have.

There was some excitement in the congregation about this line of action, although I did not share it. The sketches showed increased seating and space accommodations but at the rate that we were growing, we would soon have been in the same situation that we were trying to alleviate. In addition, an improved facility did not address all of our needs. I stated earlier that we were located on a quiet, secluded street. It was also a street that was hard to find. Visitors often mentioned in their greetings that they had finally found our church after failed attempts to locate it on previous Sunday mornings. Also, parking was becoming more of an issue for us as we had no parking lot. On-street parking was available but because of our growth, people were parking farther away, with some of them having to walk an entire city block from their cars to the church. I did not believe that remaining in our old church home was what God intended for us. But because of the relational factors detailed in previous chapters, and knowing that it would take a unified body to accomplish what the Lord had set before us, I did not stop this investigation. I didn't want to restrain the creative juices of the congregation; I merely desired to reroute them.[2]

While the steering committee pursued this path, God began giving me sermons picturing a grand cathedral of worship. God set the picture of it clearly in my mind. Every week I would find a way to communicate some exciting aspect of building our own church home. This was a wonderful time for my own faith to grow. I had a great time in the spirit, revealing to the congregation a detailed description of the church that was in my vision. I told them that God had already constructed it in the spirit realm and was simply waiting for our faith to call it into being. Hallelujah! It soon became certain that even though there was indecision in some leadership circles of the church that the pastor had a clear vision of where God wanted the church to go.[3]

I know that there is a God in heaven and that "his eye is on the sparrow." When the steering committee went to the city building department to inquire about the proposed expansion of our old church building, they were informed that in order for that to be considered, an off-street parking lot would have to be added to the plans. Many churches operate with no parking lot because they have a "grandfather variance" that excludes them from the current city codes for public use facilities. Pastors and church leaders must take note that in these cases any improvements to their facilities, especially improvements resulting in an increase in seating capacity, probably will require them to add designated off-street parking accommodations.

The only way for us to satisfy the city code would have been to purchase several of the houses on the block and convert them to a parking lot. The neighborhood residents, however, did not want to sell their properties as a survey of our neighbors quickly confirmed. This was a pivotal moment for the direction of our efforts. Our inability to purchase a church or to improve and expand on our old building resulted in a future of grace and blessing that none of us could ever have envisioned. In a meeting subsequent to these occurrences, one of the officers suggested, "Maybe we ought to look for some land." I immediately sent a member who was a real estate broker to find a suitable parcel of land for us to consider. This was the beginning of the wonderful journey that was our capital construction project. As Massey and McKinney say in *Church Administration in the Black Perspective*, "The acquisition of land is a top priority."

Stepping Out on Faith

Go from your country . . . , to the land that I will show you.
— GENESIS 12:1

The land was located on a busy corporate thoroughfare about ten minutes from our location. It was easily accessible, conveniently situated between two closely placed expressway exits. It had a much higher visibility than we enjoyed at the old site. Its size and cost fit within the faith budget of the project, and this made the parcel attractive to everyone. One evident drawback was that there was no street parking available at the site, and a parking lot was a necessary component of the construction plan. Adjacent office parking offered the hope of assistance in this area.

Another drawback that was not so evident was that the corporate development of the immediate area suggested little opportunity to acquire additional land in the future. At the time, these were secondary concerns. We now had some congregational momentum to move forward. I would advise anyone who enters into a capital project to make the continual progress of the project a priority. When a project has begun, it is usually after many prayers have been offered and great faith has been exercised. Congregational momentum and support in such major projects is priceless. Although in some cases it is unavoidable, when a project is interrupted or stalled for any reason there is a risk of incurring major damage to the spiritual life and the subsequent support from the church. Once it has begun, stopping a capital project for any reason should be avoided if at all possible. We negotiated and entered into a contract to purchase the land and began planning the actual church building.

Another divine intervention occurred that affirmed God's desire that the ministry should prosper. When we reflect on the battles and blessings of our ministerial journey, my wife and assistant pastor, Rev. Lana, often says, "God wanted this ministry and made it happen." When ministry is diligently pursued with faith, hope, and love, God's blessings are astounding. This is why we must rely on heavenly means and methods to achieve a heavenly vision. "Right relationships with God are far more important than buildings, budgets, programs, methods, church personnel, size, or anything else."[4]

While we were preparing to close on the purchase of this land parcel, another more visible and accessible parcel in the same vicinity became available. Its location was just off the main corporate avenue in a residential setting. Its attractiveness was further enhanced because it was across the street from a public park. This location was much more appealing to us. It was also adjacent to parcels of land that offered hope for future expansion. Best of all, although the land was virtually the same size in acreage and shape as the first parcel, it was being offered at over fifty thousand dollars less! *Praise God from whom all blessings flow!* We quickly paid a nominal fee to exit the previous contract and soon owned what would become the present location of DuPage African Methodist Episcopal Church. "Nobody in the world would believe that God looked after the economy for a single church, but I can show you a church that believes God did."[5]

This is an excellent juncture to mention something that is very important regarding the contract process. Our contract specified certain contingencies that protected us from foreseeable and unforeseeable problems. The contract was contingent on an acceptable soil test that would clear the site of having any hidden hazardous materials. Another contingency was that the village would approve the zoning requirements to enable the construction of our church building. Many a congregation has bought land for the purpose of constructing a new church building only to have their plans thwarted by municipal zoning restrictions. Another contingency was the requirement of a majority vote in a church conference to validate the contracts.

Many pastors and progressive church officers may look at this contingency with chagrin. There can be great anxiety generated by the prospect of any project opponents voicing their objections in the church conference. This is why I have laboriously addressed church conference and board administration in the previous chapter. As regards the contractual process, this contingency's benefit is too great to omit from the purchase agreement. It provides the congregation with a way to get out of the contract, if the Lord should suddenly lead in another direction.

The "Holy Day Inn"

Now those who were scattered went from place to place, proclaiming the word.   — ACTS 8:4

Once we had purchased land, our direction was set. We immediately proceeded with the next step of the construction process, which was the selection of an architect. Here is another insight concerning the administrative process. In our church, the trustee board has the primary responsibility for the capital project because it is responsible for the maintenance and protection of the temporal possessions of the church and the acquisition and improvement of land and buildings as approved by the church conference.[6]

As mentioned earlier, a steering committee led the project effort for the trustee board and the church. This committee consisted of five trustees selected by the pastor. I selected persons who were committed to the project and had some experience in previous capital projects, and whose leadership in the congregation was above reproach. Building an effective team is fundamental to productive organizational development.[7]

All activities related to the project were either initiated in or were processed by this committee. Any suggestions from the trustee board or the congregation at large were referred to this committee. The committee fulfilled its responsibility by prayerfully taking into account all of the information at its disposal, deliberating on it, and then making recommendations to the trustee board at the board's regularly scheduled monthly meetings. The board would receive and discuss the recommendations of the committee, sometimes sending the committee back to rework its recommendations. When committee recommendations were accepted, the committee was then authorized to take action on the recommendations. This was the basic process of administration under which the project proceeded.

A church conference was called into session only when major decisions required the church's approval. These decisions included approval of both the preliminary and final architect plans, selection of the contractor, and approval of the cost, the lender, and the loan amount. Our church conference was called into session only three times in a four-year span, from the time of our purchase of the land until our entry into the newly completed church. The ongoing life and ministry of the church was not disrupted by a preoccupation with every detail of the project. This proved satisfactory because throughout the process a constant and open flow of information continued between the trustee board and the other boards and auxiliaries. Everybody knew everything and could comment on everything. "Vision is about a preferred future. The number one job of the pastor and the leadership team is to clearly communicate the big picture." The project benefits from having the congregation included as it is led into its future.[8]

Administrative control was maintained by having formal decisions take place exclusively in the trustee board after they were processed through the steering committee. This clear and orderly process was maintained by the pastor and respected by the church leaders and the congregation. Everyone was comfortable that all things were considered in an inclusive fashion.

The selection process for the architect was done through a bidding process. We submitted the basic parameters of our project to several architectural firms, which then bid on the project. One of the firms was owned by a church member. When a church member is involved in church business that also involves outside parties, it is important that the decision making body be sensitive to any potential conflict of interest. Also, there may be a membership backlash when decisions that are in the best interests of the church body may not favor an individual member. This is a very sensitive area that requires prayerful caution whenever it arises.

We selected our architect, who then proceeded to formulate the plans for construction. Regular meetings were held between the architect and the steering committee, sometimes long into the night, as the master plan based upon "program needs, cost of construction, and availability of funds," was developed.[9] At the same time, the trustee board was authorized by the congregation to put the old church property up for sale. Our plan was to complete the architectural plans and then seek bids from construction contractors, which would come in as we were selling our old church home. We recruited a site selection committee to find a suitable, temporary home in which we could worship during construction. The committee did an excellent job.

After reviewing several options, they recommended a local Holiday Inn hotel. The hotel staff would not only set up and take down the sanctuary seating weekly but also had rooms for our Sunday school and storage for our organ, piano, and other instruments. Other options did not offer these conveniences, but were charging virtually the same price. As will soon be detailed, our stay in the Holiday Inn, which we affectionately refer to as the "Holy Day Inn," was a blessed one. We enjoyed continued good fellowship and growth even though our sojourn there was longer than we had intended. When a congregation is forced to reside in a temporary setting, it is most important that the setting be one that is highly conducive to the purpose, practices, and personality of the congregation. It is preferable that the congregation not be repeatedly uprooted and moved when it does not have a permanent location.

As I mentioned, our plan was to depart from the old church when the contracting bid was approved and to worship in our temporary location during construction. While the architect was completing our new facility plans, another congregation made an acceptable offer on our old property, which had been on the market for several months. We were relieved when this happened and rejoiced at God's perfect timing in this matter. The only stipulation was that we would have to leave our church a few months earlier than we had intended. After deliberating, we decided that the offer was one that we could not refuse, and so a great service of praise and thanksgiving was planned and held. The entire community was invited to the grand occasion. Many former members who had relocated across the country returned for this meaningful and festive event. Our bishop, the conference elders, and many ministers and friends were present. It was a grand affair. We bid a fond and faithful farewell to a location that had become an endeared spiritual home to us over the years. Little did we know that we were embarking on a journey that would sorely test our faith and fellowship.

We Were Strangers in a Strange Land

. . . You have not passed this way before.

— JOSHUA 3:4

We held our first service in the hotel, and it was a blessed worship. The Holy Spirit moved, the ministry was accommodated, and the people rejoiced. Our monthly board meetings began convening in the hotel and were often held in a dinner setting. This was a refreshing change. Choir rehearsals, weddings, and funerals were held at Second Baptist Church in Wheaton, Ilinois. We thank God for our

Christian neighbors. Many smaller group meetings were held in the homes of members. We soon negotiated with the hotel, and one of their sleeping rooms was cleared of furniture so that we could have an office. We moved in our office furniture and equipment. The secretary and myself both worked out of this office. Select small group meetings and Bible study were also held in this office. The church continued to grow, and it became evident that our prayers and faith in planning for this transition were being rewarded.

The old church property sold without a hitch. Three months after we moved into the hotel, the architect completed the plans and we let the project out for bids from contractors. Unfortunately, this was the beginning of the test of faith in this temporary, transitional circumstance. The bids came back setting the cost of construction at twice the amount that we had budgeted. This was not good at all. There was no way for us to adjust our fiscal ability for so great a disparity. In meeting with the architect, who was in all matters fair and earnest, he did not remember being told the figure that we had budgeted for church construction. In reviewing his contract, we discovered that the figure had been omitted, and even though we were sure that it had been discussed in meetings we had no documented proof.

The contractor we wished to select was immediately made aware of our circumstance, and together, along with the architect, we entered into joint discussions on how to resolve our dilemma. The Lord continued with us. Both the architect and the contractor agreed to work together, at no additional cost, to adjust the plans so that our ministry needs and budgetary constraints could both be satisfied in the project. The process, however, would not be a quick one. The work it would require of the architect and the contractor, along with the necessary reviews and approvals by both the church trustees and the village building department, would set back the groundbreaking of our new church an estimated twelve months. This would mean that instead of worshiping in the hotel for approximately one year, it would now be at least twice that long. We were not happy to receive this news. The daunting task of calling the church body together in order to share this unexpected turn of events was even more disheartening. I know now the challenge of faith in the scriptures, in Joshua 3:4, "... you have not passed this way before."

The church conference was immediately called to circumvent any wild rumors from taking root. It was imperative that we prayerfully plan ahead as a unified body while maintaining as positive a spirit as possible. Candid honesty was necessary.[10] The trustee board sat with me as the meeting convened. The prior wisdom of our administrative process again proved itself. The fact that I, as the pastor, had worked with the board and shared with the church throughout the process mitigated the feelings of frustration that surfaced. We had all been a part of things from the beginning and had proceeded together. The initial questions of why didn't we do this or that soon lost their momentum as the many inclusive instances of participation were cited. It could never be "Why didn't you?" It was always "Why didn't we?" We had done the best job that we could but there were just so many stones to turn over that we had missed one, and admittedly it was a big one. But at that point, we were all in it together. Our congregation girded itself to face the unsettling facts of our lamentable circumstance.

I must say that there are few times that I have been more affirmed in ministry. We had sold our old church and could not go back there. We were in a temporary place that represented instability, no matter how comfortable it was. And our advance to the future of God's promise was unavoidably stalled. As a congregation, we were rising to the challenge, but the prospect of this delay saddened us and sapped some of our spirit. Soon after that, I preached a sermon that reflected my feelings as pastor. The scripture was taken from Exodus 14:11–12, "Was it because there were no graves in Egypt that you have taken us away to die in the wilderness. What have you done to us, bringing us out of Egypt? Is this not the very thing we told you in Egypt, 'Let us alone and let us serve the Egyptians?' For, it would have been better for us that we served the Egyptians than to die in the wilderness." I owe the title of that sermon to a great preacher and my cousin Rev. Dr. Edward Wheeler, president of Christian Theological Seminary in Indianapolis. The sermon was entitled "One Mile from Egypt."

We were now faced with a sink-or-swim situation. Either we trusted the Lord and moved forward in faith or declined into a cesspool of projecting blame. This was a situation that threatened not only the life and the future of the congregation, but also my ministry.

My father grew up as a country boy, steeped in the folk sayings and "mother wit" (old time country wisdom) one learns growing up on a farm. When faced with a make-it-or-break-it challenge, he would recall when times got so hard on the farm that my grandpa could not purchase feed for the livestock. In times like these, Grandpa would turn the hogs loose in the woods. They would have to find roots and wild produce for themselves if they were to survive. As he watched them disappear into the trees he would whisper a saying that I heard my father repeat on more than one occasion: "It's time to root whole hog, or die poor pig." For the ministry of DuPage, it was time to root whole hog or die poor pig!

I'm happy to report that not only did our congregation rise to the challenge, but God blessed our sojourn at the Holy Day Inn abundantly. We enjoyed our fellowship greatly. New souls were added to our membership weekly. The ministry went forth unimpeded. Before we finished the eventual construction of our church, we even had to add a second Sunday morning worship service because we had outgrown the hotel ballroom.

When the day of our groundbreaking finally arrived, we enjoyed a spectacular festival of praise and worship. After the new church was completed, on the day we left the hotel we held a grand farewell worship, thanking the Lord for unmerited favor. We then drove our automobiles in a caravan to hold the first worship in our beautiful new church home. Dignitaries, family, and friends from far and near were in attendance as we marched into our sanctuary with songs of praise. The Lord is good and proved that goodness to us in ways we can never forget. But there is another part of the story that must be told, and that is the story of the financial history of our faith journey. There are many lessons in the story of our becoming the first minority group to receive a bank loan in excess of one million dollars in DuPage County, Illinois.

SIX

Financing Capital Projects

*For which of you, intending to build a tower, does not first sit down
and estimate the cost, to see whether he has enough to complete it.*

— LUKE 14:28

O UR FAITH JOURNEY in financing the building project was indeed
an interesting one. When I was first assigned to DuPage, the
finances of the church were in good condition. The church building was owned free and clear. There was a faithful group of regular
contributors, a dependable cash flow, and an established banking relationship.[1] We were located in a suburb of Chicago that had grown
considerably over the years but still retained a small-town atmosphere. Many of the residents knew each other and knew each other's
children. Most of the business owners knew most of their customers,
and our banking relationship was no exception.

Our church treasurer, Bro. Louis Garland, knew our bank's president and many of its board members. Some of them were his
neighbors. It was a pleasure for him to go into the bank each week
and make our deposits. When I was assigned as pastor, he introduced
me to many of the executives who worked at the bank. As we began
to pursue the vision of our building project, one of the first things
that we did was to meet with the appropriate people at the bank and
make them aware of our plans.

As we proceeded over the months and years with our building
program, we regularly kept the bank aware of our progress. We met
with them a couple of times a year and presented them with annual
reports. We gave them our construction budget and worked with
them in determining the borrowing ability of our church. We had
a clear understanding with the loan department of how we should

proceed and of what they could support. We felt certain that the
financial aspect of our program was well defined and under control.[2]

When we finally approved the architects' reconfigured building
plans, we approached the bank to make the formal application for
our construction loan. How true Robert Burns spoke in saying that
the best laid plans of mice and men often go astray. By a strange
twist of fate, immediately preceding the presentation of our application, our small-town neighborly bank was bought out by a large
multinational bank headquartered in downtown Chicago. This took
the management and the decision-making authority away from the
persons whom we had worked with for at least five years and put it
in the hands of total strangers who had different business priorities.

Suddenly, it appeared that no one at the bank knew how to proceed. As new faces began to appear in pivotal positions, it became
evident that the bank's process of loan application and approval
was in transition. Our worst fears concerning this matter were soon
realized. We were contacted by the bank and asked to have a representative church committee meet with an authorizing committee of
the bank on a Tuesday evening. I will never forget it, because to have
an evening meeting at the bank was highly unusual.

On the evening of the meeting, the banking committee consisted of
a few persons who were familiar to us but mostly persons from downtown Chicago whom we did not know. They reviewed our application
and listened to our presentation with interest. After answering a few
of their questions, we were informed that their response would be
forthcoming. It was not the most comfortable meeting.

In a couple of days, we received correspondence from the bank
indicating that they had approved our application, but only for 60 percent of our requested amount. When you are operating on a tight
budget and are requesting a substantial loan amount for a building
project, being short 40 percent is a lot of money. I like to say that that
bank gave us "a rejection dressed up in approval clothing." For whatever reason, we were not the target market for the new direction of
the bank. After years of planning and cultivating a relationship for
this specific purpose, we were left with nothing but a faithful effort
and a solid plan that was suddenly halted in its tracks. This is a
lesson in humility for all persons involved in God's Realm building

work. You can have all of the best intentions, intelligent preparations, and enthusiastic support but "unless the Lord builds the house, those who build it labor in vain" (Ps. 127:1a).

Grace Is Sufficient

Relief and deliverance . . . will rise from another quarter.

— ESTHER 4:14

Fortunately, God was with us. God was simply using the process of this building project to grow our faith. While we had been developing and cultivating the relationship with our primary bank, we had opened a small account with another bank. This bank was new in town, but it was a large, interstate bank. In the process of opening this small account, some of the excitement we had regarding the plans for our church was shared. Through informal conversations, bank tellers mentioned this to personal bankers who in turn mentioned it to a young, assertive commercial loan officer in that bank. He subsequently contacted me concerning our church loan business, and I met with him and discussed our future. This was three years before we would make our loan request, and at that time we were still in the planning phase and firmly committed to working with our primary bank. I communicated this in no uncertain terms to the young officer. I wanted to be totally honest with him and I was not comfortable talking with him without this being communicated.

He was not deterred in the least by this information and began what would be a three-year effort by him to secure our loan business. He made a point of cordially speaking to me whenever he saw me in the bank and always asked how things were going. He would ask for copies of the same reports that we were giving to the other bank. He would call me twice a year and invite me to lunch in very nice restaurants in order to lobby for our business. We had developed a very cordial business relationship, but I was always telling him, "You know we are applying with the other bank." He would respond, "That's what you say." I simply shared these interactions with the steering committee and the trustee board as we proceeded on our set course. We would commend his efforts, but we all knew that he had little chance of being successful, or so we thought.

I don't know if he was an angel sent by God for our deliverance, or if he was just a keen business person. I only know that when we received the disappointing correspondence concerning our loan application from what had been our primary bank, my immediate response was to tell the board that I was going to meet with the young banker. Because of having to adjust our architectural plans, we had already been twice as long in the hotel as we had originally intended. Time was now of the essence and this other bank represented the only financial institution that had information on our finances and the project. There was no place else that we could make an immediate application for a construction loan.

I called him the next morning to make an appointment, and he agreed to meet with me. I shared with him all that had occurred and told him quite candidly, "If you really want our business, this is your chance." He immediately took our loan application and informed me of his bank's loan approval procedure. Our church supplied him with all of the updated documents he requested, and he submitted our application to the appropriate committee. Within a month of our "disqualifying approval" from our now former primary bank, we received an "unqualified approval" for the complete amount of our loan request from our new primary bank. How well William Cowper wrote in his beautiful poem:

> God moves in mysterious ways,
> His wonders to perform.
> He plants his footsteps on the seas,
> and rides above the storm!

Needless to say, the small account we had opened there immediately swelled with our building fund, which was transferred from the other bank. DuPage County is situated west and adjacent to Cook County, where Chicago is located. African Americans are only 3 percent of the total population of DuPage County.

DuPage AME Church was the first African American group to receive a loan in excess of one million dollars from a bank in DuPage County. The president of our lending bank's commercial department commemorated the occasion by proudly presenting Bro. Garland and me with engraved Cross pens. We used them to sign the final documents. This was a great day of victory and rejoicing for our congregation. As Rev. Lana said, "The Lord wanted this ministry."

There is some blessed irony that ends the story of this initial and quite educational foray of our church into the world of financing major projects. Approximately six months after the closing of our loan, the small community bank that previously had been our primary bank and had been bought out by the large downtown Chicago bank, was again bought out and acquired by another banking corporation. You will never guess who bought out the bank that would not approve the loan amount we requested. It was the bank that subsequently did approve our loan request, which was now our primary bank. And that is not the complete irony. In the new reorganization that was occurring at that bank, our loan servicing file was assigned back to one of the old loan officers of the original small-town bank. He was one of the few persons who had been with us from the beginning of our discussions on financing the project. He had also been present at that fateful Tuesday evening meeting with the downtown committee. The first time I walked back into that familiar office and shook his hand, his only words were, "Reverend, you got the victory."

I was more than happy to correct his sincere compliment by saying, "No, sir, the Lord got it!"

The Loan Application Package

The man questioned us carefully.

— GENESIS 43:7A

For secular business purposes, a church is considered a not-for-profit corporation. The church members are considered its volunteer donor base. Many municipalities will classify a church building that is being newly constructed as a "special use facility" as opposed to simply a "public use facility." These distinctions mean that a church must be prepared to present itself in a way peculiar to its unique identity when seeking financing. Lending institutions usually require information about the church beyond that of its financial records. There is a specific order and some fundamental components of a church's financial application package that can greatly enhance a church's probability of achieving loan approval.

The package should begin with a summary statement page indicating the loan amount and the purpose for the loan. Pastors and church officers must remember that a bank is in the business of making good loans. It is not in the business of forwarding ministry. The banker can more readily review your application information after first knowing what you are asking for and why. This is the initial information the bank needs. The stated amount and purpose for the loan will reveal if the loan request falls within the parameters of the bank's business policies and that will tell the bank what benefit it may receive through the loan transaction. Again I emphasize, the bank is first and foremost a business institution and not a community service agency. The bank is primarily interested in the profit potential of the transaction.

The package should continue with a personal vita or résumé of the pastor and the chief officers. The church is a corporate entity, but the bank wants to know the primary individuals it is dealing with. These are the persons who will share the legal responsibility for signing on and paying for the loan. If the loan request falls within the parameters of the bank's policies, then the bank will have some experience in dealing with church loans. It will understand the transient nature of the pastorate, and it will be wary of the potential volatility of the congregational setting. Many bank officers themselves are officers in their own respective churches, and they have experienced problems with the pastor and the congregation. They will be as interested in the primary people involved in the loan obligation as they will be in the church's history, its organization, and even its fiscal ability, which is subject to change.

The loan package itself should be as professional a presentation as possible. A package that is neat, organized, and even bound emphasizes the ability of the church to undertake the loan. Architectural renderings of the proposed construction along with pictures of the pastor and officers will enhance the package's professional look while also serving to further familiarize the bank with its potential customer. Establishing familiarity facilitates a comfort level between the bank and church contact persons as discussions on the transaction proceed.

A complete church directory of the membership with names and addresses should be added. The financing agency will want documentation that confirms the total membership of the church because the membership represents the resource pool from which the funds to repay the loan will come. It is expected that the pastor and the church officers will be excited about the project. The application package, however, must emphasize the entire church's willingness to meet the loan obligation. Sharing the church directory not only satisfies this requirement but also indicates that the church is united behind the project. The potential growth of the congregation as a result of the project will not be the bank's primary consideration for approving the loan. They will be interested in growth for future reference, but banks and most reputable lending institutions are conservative financial corporations. They are in the business of making good loans and are not in the business of making bad loans and then foreclosing on bad loans. Presenting the church directory will emphasize the church's ability to meet the loan payments.

Another benefit of producing the personal vita of the church principals, along with the church directory, is the clear indication this gives the bank that the church has nothing to hide. This sets a tone of honesty, which will cast a favorable light on the bank's scrutiny of the church's financial records. A tone of openness can pay great dividends as the bank weighs its decision on whether to grant the church's loan request. The membership should be informed of the process and encouraged to support the project should they be contacted by the bank. This gives each member a greater sense of ownership of the project and solidifies his or her financial support by creating the anticipation of this broader contribution to the project. It also serves to bind any contrary spirits that may be circling around the project by this illuminating inclusion of everyone in the process. Evil spirits find great difficulty in operating where there is light.

The church history can be the next component presented in the package. It should be written to show the church's progress, growth, and other positive strides. The ministerial efforts of the church may be recounted, but remember the bank is not so much interested in the good work that the church is doing unless the good work relates to the church's ability to repay the loan. For the purposes of gaining loan approval, the highlighting of significant people who have previously passed through the church will not be important unless they are characterized as models of the current church membership's ability to repay the loan. The church may have many illustrious figures in its history, but those persons are no longer there to repay the loan. Citing instances of recent personal sacrifices on the part of current church members, however, is particularly effective.

When the bank has seen what is being requested and who is making the request, the church history can begin to fill in the blanks and inform the bank in some of its other areas of inquiry. No matter what formula the bank uses to consider loan applications, it always must be satisfied in three basic areas of qualification. These are not grounded in the worthiness of the church's cause or in the goodness of its people. A loan application is a business transaction, and the bank's concerns are primarily financial. The three basic areas of a bank's loan qualification process are: (1) the ability of the applicant to repay the loan; (2) the stability of the applicant indicated by residence history, employment, or operation; (3) and the willingness of the applicant as regards the applicant's credit history.

At this point, the financial reports of the church can be presented. The reports should reflect at least a three-year history of the church's receipts and expenditures. These reports should be as detailed as possible, including copies of all pertinent bank statements and related documents. The detail suggested in this component of the loan application package highlights the basic goal of any loan application, which is to provide all of the answers that the lending agency may have concerning the request within the body of the application itself. The loan application should be comprehensive in the presentation of the church's finances. It should include every conceivable piece of information that may be requested by the lending agency.

The pastor and the church officers should not have to verbally explain anything concerning the church finances. Their elaboration on any point of information should be minimal. The perfect application has everything in the reports and the applicant parties should be able to answer any questions by saying, "If you will refer to page number _____ you will see _____ " and so on. This is the most professional way to request monies from a lending agency and demonstrate the business acumen of the church. An application presented in this manner strengthens the request by communicating that the church is in control of its finances. If the pastor and officers have to do a lot of talking to convince the loan officer or committee as to the application's worthiness, then the probability of the loan application being approved will diminish. The financial reports must be comprehensive and thorough. They should present the sure capability of the church to repay the loan. Of course, the church must keep good records to make such a presentation. If you are considering such an application in the future and your church finances are not reflected in regular, line item records, begin now in making and keeping detailed weekly, monthly, and annual financial records.

The financial component of the application must include a detailed presentation of how the money being requested will be used. This is where the construction project itself is presented in detail, specifying the architect and presenting the architect's résumé; specifying the contractor and presenting the contractor's résumé; outlining the construction budget; and providing the plans, drawings, construction timeline, construction permit process, and any other significant information. The lenders want to know more than to whom they are giving the money; they also want to know how it will be spent. Again, the applicant's goal is to answer all of the lender's questions about the project within the body of the application. Upon being asked any question by a loan officer, the pastor and the church officers should be able to refer to a certain page or section of the application and then add a minimal elaboration in response. Being able to do this will impress the lender with the church's detailed preparation for the loan request as well as for the project itself.

The application should show how the loan will be repaid. The package should include a church budget of financial projections for at least three years following the loan approval. This will be a budget projection that is both comprehensive and realistic. By comprehensive I mean that it should take into account all of the anticipated expenses of the church, including expenses that the church may not currently have. The new mortgage on the completed facility and the projected

CHURCH BUDGET
Sample A

CASH RECEIPTS	JAN	FEB	MAR	APR	MAY	JUNE	JULY	AUG	SEPT	OCT	NOV	DEC	Y-T-D		
TITHES	0	0	0	0	0	0	0	0	0	0	0	0	0		
GENERAL FUND	0	0	0	0	0	0	0	0	0	0	0	0	0		
BUILDING FUND	0	0	0	0	0	0	0	0	0	0	0	0	0		
MISSIONS FUND	0	0	0	0	0	0	0	0	0	0	0	0	0		
SUNDAY SCHOOL	0	0	0	0	0	0	0	0	0	0	0	0	0		
CONFERENCE CLAIMS	0	0	0	0	0	0	0	0	0	0	0	0	0		
ANNIVERSARY	0	0	0	0	0	0	0	0	0	0	0	0	0		
WOMEN'S DAY	0	0	0	0	0	0	0	0	0	0	0	0	0		
WOMEN'S MINISTRY	0	0	0	0	0	0	0	0	0	0	0	0	0		
MEN'S DAY	0	0	0	0	0	0	0	0	0	0	0	0	0		
DESIGNATED-AFTER OFFERING	0	0	0	0	0	0	0	0	0	0	0	0	0		
DESIGNATED-BOOKS	0	0	0	0	0	0	0	0	0	0	0	0	0		
DESIGNATED-ORGANIZATIONS	0	0	0	0	0	0	0	0	0	0	0	0	0		
DESIGNATED-OTHER	0	0	0	0	0	0	0	0	0	0	0	0	0		
INTEREST	0	0	0	0	0	0	0	0	0	0	0	0	0		
NEW CHAPEL OF FAITH	0	0	0	0	0	0	0	0	0	0	0	0	0		
FOOD PANTRY	0	0	0	0	0	0	0	0	0	0	0	0	0		
SUMMER CAMP	0	0	0	0	0	0	0	0	0	0	0	0	0		
TREE OF LIFE	0	0	0	0	0	0	0	0	0	0	0	0	0		
RETURNED CHECK PAYMENTS	0	0	0	0	0	0	0	0	0	0	0	0	0		
TOTAL RECEIPTS	0	0	0	0	0	0	0	0	0	0	0	0	0		

CASH DISBURSEMENTS	JAN	FEB	MAR	APR	MAY	JUNE	JULY	AUG	SEPT	OCT	NOV	DEC	Y-T-D	BUDG	% BUDG
STEWARD BOARD													0		
TRUSTEE BOARD													0		
CONFERENCE CLAIMS													0		
CONNECTIONAL													0		
**SUMMER CAMP													0		
**SUNDAY SCHOOL													0		
MUSIC DEPARTMENT													0		
ACCAPELLA/ANTHEM CHOIRS													0		
**GOSPEL CHOIR													0		
VOICES OF TOMORROW													0		
**SUNBEAM/INSPIRATIONAL CHOIRS													0		
VOICES OF PRAISE													0		
**MISSIONARY													0		
YPD													0		
GIRL SCOUTS													0		
BOY SCOUTS													0		
HEALTH MINISTRY													0		
USHER BOARD													0		
**ANNIVERSARY													0		
**WOMEN'S DAY													0		
WOMEN'S MINISTRY													0		
**MEN'S DAY													0		
LAY ORGANIZATION													0		
**BANK CHARGES													0		
DESIGNATED-ORGANIZATIONS													0		
DESIGNATED-OTHER													0		
CLASS LEADERS													0		
**MORTGAGE - 4300 YACKLEY													0		
**MORTGAGE - 2000 WARRENVILLE													0		
**MORTGAGE - 2010 WARRENVILLE													0		
**MORTGAGE - 2014 WARRENVILLE													0		
NEW PROPERTY													0		
LEGAL FEES													0		
**PROPERTY TAXES													0		
TREE OF LIFE/CHAPEL OF FAITH													0		
SPECIAL PROGRAMS													0		
SAVINGS													0		
BUDGET ADJUSTMENT													0		
TOTAL DISBURSEMENTS	0	0	0	0	0	0	0	0	0	0	0	0	0	0	0%

maintenance costs, such as utilities, are examples of such expenses. There are certain recurring expenses that will continue as well as others that will be adjusted to apply to the new location. The budget projection should be realistic in that it should extrapolate the figures of the budgets of the previously presented finance reports. Although there can be an indication of the anticipated increase in receipts as a

CHURCH BUDGET
Sample B

2006 STEWARD BOARD DISBURSEMENTS BALANCE SHEET															
ACCOUNT	JAN	FEB	MAR	APR	MAY	JUNE	JULY	AUG	SEPT	OCT	NOV	DEC	Y-T-D	BUDGET	% BUDGET
PASTOR'S SALARY															
PASTOR'S PENSION															
PASTOR'S INSURANCE (MED.)															
PASTOR'S SOCIAL SECURITY															
PASTOR'S TRAVEL															
PASTOR'S CAR ALLOWANCE															
PASTOR'S LIFE INSURANCE															
PASTOR'S ANNUITY															
PASTOR'S CONTINUING ED															
CONFERENCE EXPENSE															
MINISTERIAL STAFF															
SALARY-MUSICIANS															
VESTMENTS															
PRESIDING ELDER															
DELEGATE'S EXPENSE															
REACH															
POOR STEWARDS															
BENEVOLENT															
ALTAR FLOWERS															
N. DIST. CONFERENCE															
ECONOMIC CONF. EXPENSE															
PR-NEWSPAPERS															
PR-ORGANIZATIONS															
PR-OTHER															
BOOKS/PUBLICATIONS															
OUTREACH															
PROGRAM-OTHER															
PROGRAM-FELLOWSHIP															
PROGRAM-COMMUNION/BAPTISM															
LOVE GIFT-ORGANIZATION															
LOVE GIFT-CONNECTIONAL															
LOVE GIFT-SPEAKER															
MISC-STEWARDS															
RETURNED CHECKS															
ACCOUNTING FEES															
	0	0	0	0	0	0	0	0	0	0	0	0	0	0	0%

result of the new project, it should have some continuity with the existing church budget.[3] The lender will view any anticipated increase as speculation until the project is completed and the increase is realized. When the loan is approved, it will be approved based upon the church's ability to repay the loan prior to the project's completion and not upon what the church will realize after the project's completion.

CHURCH BUDGET
Sample C

2006 TRUSTEE BOARD DISBURSEMENTS SHEET															
ACCOUNT	JAN	FEB	MAR	APR	MAY	JUNE	JULY	AUG	SEPT	OCT	NOV	DEC	Y-T-D	BUDG	% BUDG
PART TIME OFFICE ASST													0		
SALARY - ACCTS PAYABLE MGR													0		
OFFICE ASSISTANT													0		
SALARY-OFFICE ADM													0		
SALARY-EXEC ASSISTANT													0		
SHUTTLE DRIVER													0		
AUDIO TECHNICAL													0		
AUDIO TECH ASST													0		
MEDIA EDITOR													0		
HEALTH INSURANCE (Office Administrator)													0		
UMBRELLA INSURANCE (PROPERTY/LIAB)													0		
SALARY FACILITY MANAGER													0		
SALARY PART-TIME CUSTODIAN													0		
CUSTODIAL SERVICE													0		
CHURCH UTILITIES - ELECTRICITY													0		
CHURCH UTILITIES - GAS													0		
CHURCH UTILITIES - WATER													0		
CHURCH UTILITIES - PHONE													0		
CHURCH UTILITIES - REFUSE													0		
FIRE ALARM													0		
MEDIA (FORMERLY AUDIO/VIDEO)													0		
RPR/MAINT TRANSPORTATION													0		
CHURCH OPERATIONS - EQUIP RNTL													0		
CHURCH OPERATIONS - SUPPLIES													0		
CHURCH - SNOW REMOVAL													0		
CHURCH - LAWN CARE													0		
CHURCH REPAIRS/MAINT-4300 YACKLEY													0		
REPAIR MAINT-2000 WARRENVILLE													0		
REPAIR MAINT-2010 WARRENVILLE													0		
REPAIR MAINT-2014 WARRENVILLE													0		
AUDIO EQUIPMENT													0		
COMPUTER SYSTEM													0		
HOUSING ALLOWANCE													0		
PRINTING-OUTSIDE, XEROX METER													0		
MISC. TRUSTEES													0		
MISCELLANEOUS SUBSCRIPTIONS													0		
POSTAGE													0		
	0	0	0	0	0	0	0	0	0	0	0	0	0	0	0%
MORTGAGE 4300 YACKLEY													0		
MORTGAGE 2000 WARRENVILLE													0		
MORTGAGE 2010 WARRENVILLE													0		
MORTGAGE 2014 WARRENVILLE													0		

Let me reiterate this salient point. The bank will not approve a loan request based on budget projections. The bank will approve the loan request only if the church is able to pay the mortgage amount based upon the church's receipts at the time the application is filed. Showing inordinate amounts of future increases in receipts may be viewed by the lender as overzealous and irresponsible. Most lenders are conservative money managers who base loan decisions on current receipts. The bank does not make loans based on faith projections; the bank makes loans based on current facts and figures. Also keep in mind that banks don't normally lend money to those who need it. They tend to lend it to those who want it but can get it from another source. Make your loan application package attractive so that the bank you present it to will want your business before you give it to some other lender.

Any other supporting data concerning the stability, ability, and willingness of the church to repay the loan is a welcome addition to the bare statistics of the church's finances. This information should include, but not be limited to, growth statistics; ministry outreach; congregational programs; corporate, political, and community group affiliations; and any information that helps cast the church in a stable, progressive, and positive light. Providing a holistic picture of the total life and ministry of the church will have some influence on the loan committee when it gets to its final deliberations. Just remember that although ministry is primary for the very existence of the church, it is secondary to a lending institution, whose primary concern is the church's ability to repay the loan.

The information in this chapter has proven advantageous on several occasions when we have sought funding for various projects. The geographic location of a church, the socioeconomics of its community, the type of project it is undertaking, and many other factors pertaining to the specific situation of a church can also affect the funding request. At DuPage, we have been very successful in processing several funding requests through many different funding venues and have found the aforementioned strategies to be highly effective.

The Church Capital Campaign

Take from among you an offering to the Lord; let whoever is of a generous heart bring the Lord's offering. — EXODUS 35:5

When a church decides to undertake a major construction project, the spiritual disciplines should be invoked to petition God's divine direction and provision. Prayer meetings, Bible studies, church-wide fasts,

CHURCH BUSINESS LOAN APPLICATION

Basic Components Checklist

❑ Loan request amount and purpose

❑ Pastor and chief officers' vitae

❑ Church membership directory

❑ Church history

❑ Previous three years line item finance reports

❑ Budget for loan amount usage (project budget)

❑ Three-year line item finance projections

❑ Miscellaneous support information

Loan package should be neat, orderly,
and professionally compiled.

---

and special worship services all assist in maintaining the church's Christian priorities as it pursues its envisioned destiny. The stewardship discipline of giving tithes and offerings is the best foundation for any church's fiscal endeavors. It is difficult for a congregation to attempt a major project that requires an increased financial commitment when it has not come to an understanding, acceptance, and practice of the discipline of tithing. Tithing should be a fundamental component in every Christian faith walk. It will take great faith for the congregation to withstand the many unforeseen emergencies, setbacks, demonic attacks, etc., and hold together through the course of the project. Even after the new church building is completed, the transition of moving the membership from one location to another will itself be a traumatic change. The new facility will be able to accommodate new ministries and the congregation will demand them. The initiation of these will be quite chaotic at points. The more spiritually mature the congregation is, the easier it will make these adjustments.

The stewardship of tithes and offerings is a visible gauge of the congregation's spiritual maturity. Christian stewardship evidences the faith that such a monumental undertaking will require. "And without faith it is impossible to please God; for whoever would approach him must believe that he exists and that he rewards those who seek him" (Heb. 11:6). So the spiritual growth and health of a congregation, as indicated by their stewardship, must be the first and primary concern of any pastor and group of officers who are attempting to lead a congregation in a major project.

Establishing an ongoing stewardship commitment in the church is the best way to ensure the victory of the capital project. The congregation, however, usually will have to accept the challenge of an additional financial sacrifice. In the history of the church, many small fund-raisers, programs, dinners, bake sales, etc., have been used when the church needed more money. Stewardship is the biblical means of supporting the church's ministry. It is also the perfect vehicle to grow the congregation spiritually during a major project like a capital campaign. During a capital campaign the relevance of tithing is clearly illustrated. Small fund-raisers are good for youth ministries and various programs are wonderful for congregational fellowship, but a construction project may total as much as two or three times the church's total annual receipts. In such cases, the church may consider a major fund-raiser or some campaign through which to receive a substantial percentage of the funds needed to complete the project. A capital fund-raising campaign is highly recommended in this situation.

A capital fund-raising campaign is a special drive or event by the church that will net a significant portion of the money needed to complete the capital project. Most lending institutions require the church to provide a substantial percentage of the amount as a contingency of their funding approval. Twenty percent of the total project budget is a good average of the minimum the church will be expected to raise. Ideally, the church should have most of this money when it presents its loan application. The bank will not be impressed by what the church is going to do. Remember, the bank deals in the facts of what the church actually has, not what the church anticipates having. The bank is not in the business of showing faith. It is in the business of making a profit. Nor is the bank in the business of taking chances.

It is in the business of investing in projects with a high probability of success. The bank is not in the business of collecting on bad loans. That is simply an undesirable necessity of their business. The bank is in the business of making what it considers to be good loans. Many churches struggle through the process of acquiring funding to support their projects simply because they do not understand this basic reality. The bank is not a faith institution. The church is a faith institution. The bank is a financial institution and the language it speaks is not one of faith, but one of finances. The church may raise the funds it needs through its exercise of godly faith, but it then must present to the bank what it has raised as a testament, and not as an argument, of its faith.

It is true that a sincere and well articulated plea can be presented to a lending institution. It is not inappropriate to challenge a lending institution to partnership in a worthy project, especially when that project will benefit the community in which the lending institution does business. It is good business for banks and lending institutions to invest in their community. A lending institution, however, is unlikely to approve funding for a major project on the strength of a heartfelt challenge. The recommendations in this chapter, in the great majority of cases, will work nearly every time. Any good leader, or group of leaders, owes it to God and their constituency to give their church the best chance for victory.

The campaign should not only be aggressive enough to net a significant percentage of the total project amount, but it should also be singular in its approach in that when it is completed, there is no further need for special fund-raising for the project. After the capital campaign the church should be able to finish the project with tithes and offerings.

This can be accomplished because usually there is an added energy in the congregation generated by the project that strengthens the tithing discipline. The campaign should be planned in a way that makes it inclusive and gives everyone in the congregation the opportunity to participate on some level. Having a privileged few doing most of the giving to the exclusion of other church members who are not as financially well off should be avoided. When the officers of DuPage and I discussed our need for a major intake of funds, we first did a thorough analysis of the financial demographics of our church family. We then determined to have a giving campaign that would request varying amounts and allow a feasible period of time for persons to fulfill their commitment. We also wanted the "offerings" to be visibly acknowledged in some way, both as an encouragement of participation and as a historic testament of the contributor's faith. We looked at many different vendors who offered this type of vehicle and agreed upon what we call "The Tree of Life."

The Tree of Life is an everlasting testimonial of the faith of the participants. It visibly preserves their participation in the display of a tree replica that is placed in a highly visible area in the church. The campaign was discussed by a volunteer committee and presented to the various boards of the church prior to its kickoff at our annual church conference. This allowed for the church leaders to have input in its development and to take ownership of the campaign. It also gave them an opportunity to pray about their pledge so that they would be prepared to assume a leadership role in leading the church in the campaign.

The campaign offered the opportunity for persons to participate by contributing $250, $500, $1,000, $2,000 or $5,000. There was a pledge period offered to give the members time to select and to make their commitments. The pledge period was two months and occurred during a time when no other major activities were going on in the church. During the pledge period of the campaign, every week at the regular worship services a committee member would make an announcement and an appeal to the congregation. This appeal was a summarized version of the initial appeal that was made at the church conference. A table was conveniently accessible outside of the sanctuary where pledges could be received each Sunday. When the pledge period was completed, a four-month payment period followed, where the persons who had made pledges could then pay their pledges.

A flexible payment plan was available. It was emphasized in the beginning that the pledge was not to be viewed as a legal contract between the member and the church, but rather a spiritual covenant between that person or family and God. Our pledge period was November and December. Our payment period was from the beginning of the year to Easter Sunday. During the payment period, announcements were also made by the committee, but they were not made as frequently. Planned monthly correspondence from the church to

CAPITAL CAMPAIGN FINANCE PLAN

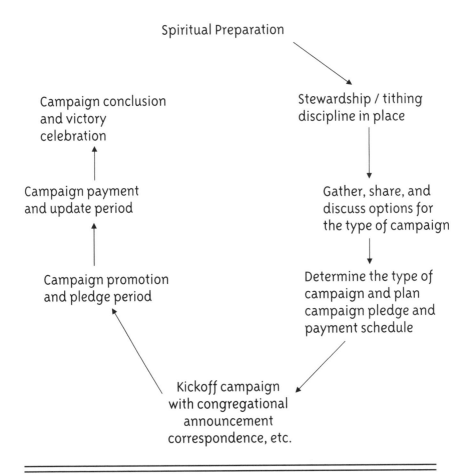

Spiritual Preparation

Campaign conclusion and victory celebration

Stewardship / tithing discipline in place

Campaign payment and update period

Gather, share, and discuss options for the type of campaign

Campaign promotion and pledge period

Determine the type of campaign and plan campaign pledge and payment schedule

Kickoff campaign with congregational announcement correspondence, etc.

the members supported the campaign from kickoff to completion. A table to receive payments was readily accessible outside of the sanctuary every Sunday, but the various payment options also included paying the pledge during the regular offering with a special pledge designation on the church offering envelopes so that the payment was properly recorded. Pledges were also received by mail and through online donation.

I am happy to say that the congregation wholeheartedly supported our capital campaign efforts and we were successful in meeting the campaign goals. The Tree of Life now stands as a beautiful presentation of the faith God's people exercised for the building of our church. There are many different ways to conduct a capital fundraising campaign, which range from other in-house ideas to retaining outside and professional consultation. I advise that the pastor and church leaders pray diligently, seek advice from trusted sources, and consider all of the options available to them in determining their direction concerning any capital fund-raising campaign.[4] The points to emphasize are that it be a campaign that the entire church can participate in and that it be planned to allow for the best opportunity for the participants to make and meet their pledges.

SEVEN

Worship

Ascribe to the Lord the glory due his name;
bring an offering and come before him.
Worship the Lord in holy splendor.
— 1 CHRONICLES 16:29

WORSHIP, AND MORE SPECIFICALLY Sunday morning worship, is the most important activity of the church. When we talk about going to church, we are generally referring to attending the Sunday morning service. We might miss something during the week and say, "I missed rehearsal" or "I missed the meeting." But if we don't go to the Sunday service, we say, "I missed church!" To highlight this point, when we speak of evangelism, we are most often referring to inviting people to Sunday service. Theologically, we could argue that the Sunday worship service is the anchor for all of the church's ministries and activities. "Remember the Sabbath Day, to keep it Holy" (Exod. 20:8). Many churches today have weekly worship services that are not on Sunday morning, but the point emphasized here is not the day of the worship but that worship itself is the primary church function. In order to create a vibrant church, worship must be the priority.[1]

This chapter could easily have been the first chapter of this book because worship is the central activity of the church. All of the progressive programs in the world won't sustain a church's vibrancy and foster a growing and thriving congregation if the worship does not facilitate a personal connection between the worshiper and God. Unfortunately, this is not the case in many churches today.[2] This chapter will present certain faith challenges for which the previous chapters have served as prerequisites.

Churches that are without growth and vibrancy today are generally churches that are not connecting the worshiper with God. Their worship services are not dynamic. They offer no anticipation or opportunity for an intervention of the Holy Spirit. They are predictable in the routine of their order of worship. In *The Purpose-Driven Church*, Rick Warren says, "Predictability has killed more worship services than any other factor." In such worship services, something new, exciting, unexpected, and surprising almost never happens. In fact, the worship itself is geared to keep any new and lively occurrences from taking place. The setting is sedate and the atmosphere is subdued. This is the perfect format for a prayer meeting, but it is a disastrous format for praise and worship.

To be fair, subdued worship, particularly in the African American community, served congregations well in years past. Such worship showed dignity and sophistication. It validated the education and refined culture that proved the intelligence of the people. These paradigms, however, have long since served their purpose and cease to be the need or the priority of today's generation. Today's worshiping generation feels "no need to belong to some group of old ladies singing irrelevant hymns to a droning organ, sitting in uncomfortable pews, and listening to a judgmental treatise on some finer point of theology that has nothing to do with paying this month's rent, keeping children off drugs, or repairing fractured self-esteem."[3]

This chapter will present several clear and practical suggestions regarding worship along with a feasible process of implementing them for the purpose of revitalizing the congregation. By feasible I mean that the suggestions are offered to facilitate dynamism without alienating the members who are rooted and grounded in the traditional worship framework. The goal of this chapter is to assist a church that wants to become more dynamic in doing so, being careful in a manner that is spiritually healthy for the entire congregation. What is desired is to create a worship service that is attractive to middle age and young families, couples, and individuals. This can be accomplished without alienating the older members who have been the bedrock of the congregation for many years and continue to be its strongest supporters.[4] Does this sound impossible? Good!

That means it is a job for God and we know that "for mortals it is impossible, but for God all things are possible!" (Matt. 19:26).

The Worship Setting

. . . First be reconciled to your brother or sister, and then come and offer your gift.   — MATTHEW 5:24B

In order to provide a worship setting that is conducive to warmth, vibrancy, and growth, we must connect with the worshipers even before they enter the sanctuary. By the time they enter the sanctuary, they have awakened, dressed, gotten out of the house, driven to the church, parked, and entered the church building. Any number of deterrents can occur to the most faithful saints between the time they initially "woke up with their mind stayed on Jesus" and later arrived at church. It therefore behooves the church congregation to make the arrival of the worshiper as spiritually uplifting as possible. Interestingly enough, this does not begin with the members or the worship service itself. This begins with the church's buildings and grounds. The appearance, or curb appeal, of the worship facility, particularly its landscaping "frequently contributes greatly to a sense of welcome and invitation."[5]

Regardless of the location of the church or the financial situation of the congregation, the care and maintenance of the church property must be a priority. When a defect in the building or grounds, like a bare patch of lawn or peeling paint, is first seen, it is easily noticed. After that defect, however, has been seen numerous times it is no longer noticed. That means that there may be defects and eyesores in any facility that the officers and members are not noticing but that visitors and prospective members are noticing. The officers and members must constantly make the maintenance and care of their property a part of the culture of their congregation. For setting a vibrant worship tone, manicured lawns and freshly painted walls are a good beginning.

Now we come to a most crucial issue in the contemporary worship setting and that is the provision of adequate parking. Kennon L. Callahan says in *Twelve Keys to an Effective Church*, "Parking capacity and convenience is a decisive factor in attendance, participation, and giving." When a church sanctuary is built, the governing municipality generally requires a certain number of parking spaces according to the member of seats in the sanctuary. The general ratio has been one space for every three seats. Even this number of spaces, however, could be inadequate for the worshiping family today. In today's society, a family does not always drive to church together. Sometimes wives, husbands, and even teenagers come in separate cars. Parking is a big issue and a vibrant church must invest in providing adequate parking for its congregation. Each space will pay for itself many times over.[6]

Sometimes land is not available to be used for parking. This is the case with many older churches. In such cases, there are still options available so that the church may provide a warm welcome to arriving worshipers and also relieve the frustration of inadequate parking. One option is to develop a parking ministry. A parking ministry places courteous attendants outside of the church to assist the worshipers as they arrive. It also provides another ministry where church members may give service. As we have already discussed, participation in the life and service of the church, through its various ministries, is the best way to retain regularly attending members.

Another way to address a parking issue is to start another service. This is probably the most challenging suggestion because it involves the worshiping life of the church. Starting a new service, however, is recommended whenever the church attendance for seating or parking capacity reaches 80 percent.[7] Another service automatically doubles the available parking space. When DuPage's 8:00 a.m. Sunday service neared overflow capacity for parking, we agreed together to begin a 7:00 a.m. service. We set the time of the following two services back fifteen minutes. This was done primarily to accommodate parking rather than seating. This very early service now has a regular and growing number of loyal attendees. I am also happy to report that at this writing, our 8:15 a.m. service has again reached capacity in parking. So now we have started a shuttle service to ferry members regularly between a parking lot that is near but not adjacent to the church. This shuttle service immediately caught on and is becoming more popular. We make sure that it is regular, dependable, and comfortable.

Starting a new service can also increase the church's evangelistic outreach. In *How to Start a New Service,* Charles Arn states, "More services mean more visitors and more visitors mean more members."

Our contemporary culture promotes the recommendation to have not only multiple services and surplus parking but also childcare.[8] Because we want to train children to sit in worship, DuPage's Youth Church does not operate during the entire worship service. It begins just before the music selection that precedes the sermon. This allows for the childcare volunteers to share in a part of the worship on their particular day of service.

The easier it is for worshipers to park, the more worshipers we will have, and the better their spirits will be as they enter the sanctuary. DuPage has a shuttle service, a parking ministry, a hospitality ministry with greeters who welcome the worshipers at the door, and an usher board in order to facilitate as warm a welcome into the church as possible.

Worship Tempo

> *These things I remember,*
> *as I pour out my soul:*
> *how I went with the throng,*
> *and led them in procession to the house of God,*
> *with glad shouts and songs of thanksgiving.*
> — PSALM 42:4

There is one characteristic of worship that can change the entire direction of a congregation from being lethargic to being dynamic: the worship must be *upbeat.* There should be an upbeat tempo along with smooth transitions between worship components as they flow from one to another.[9] The introit, hymn selections, and even the speaking and reading components should exude a tempo and tenor that are upbeat and lively.

WELCOME MINISTRIES

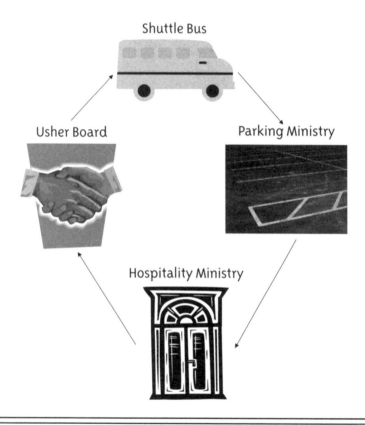

Shuttle Bus

Usher Board

Parking Ministry

Hospitality Ministry

As the spoken word has just been mentioned, I will here interject a most important warning of which every pulpiteer should take heed, namely, that talking kills the spirit in worship. Worship should primarily or even wholly consist of spiritual components (i.e., praise, prayer, singing, etc.). Unless there is a liturgical reading or the sermon is being preached or taught, communal aspects of announcements and other remarks not directly related to worship should be reduced, and in some cases eliminated. Worship leaders and participants often spend a lot of time in worship speaking on subjects that are interesting to the speaker and even interesting or humorous to the congregation but are not elicitations of divine worship. As regards the divine worship of Holy God, this speaking acts to "quench the Spirit" and thereby diminishes the dynamic effect of worship.

By no means should any official, internal church business occur during worship services![10] Please do not use the service of godly worship as an official board meeting. Some might say that this is the only time the members are present to hear important information. I would encourage that the purity of worship be preserved and that a proper church meeting be called at another time, preferably not on Sunday. Administrative church business should be addressed outside of worship.

I know that to some these suggestions of initiating a more upbeat tempo, reducing the communal announcements, and eliminating all references to official church business may seem utterly impractical. To you I have this most serious and sincere question: What is more important to you, the traditional style of worship and music, or your children and grandchildren coming to church? This chapter will proceed with a series of suggestions that are widely practiced in a multitude of vibrant congregations. What we are really dealing with is not the style of worship, but rather with a much greater challenge: the challenge to change, and we might as well meet the challenge head on.

The inability of many congregations to implement new ideas and concepts indicates a spiritual insufficiency. In most cases, personal insecurity reveals our spiritual immaturity, which is evidenced by our inability to follow the leading of the Holy Spirit. It is obvious that many congregations are loosing members and have fewer resources to conduct ministry. It is just as obvious that other congregations are thriving and have seemingly unlimited resources. What is the difference? For the purpose of this chapter, let's look at worship. I am certain that in most cases, failing congregations have worships that are routine in their order, offering little in spiritual stimulation to their worshipers. Most dynamic congregations have a lively worship that generates anticipation of something new and different occurring every week. Let me relay a personal experience to emphasize my point.

I have attended some high school sports contests and witnessed a great unfairness. I have seen a coach lose a game by benching the player who could win the game in order to play the coach's son or some other favorite but less talented player. That coach cared more about his own personal agenda than about the welfare of the team and the school. That coach would rather play a favorite player and lose than play the more talented player and win the game. To me, this is absolutely unfathomable, and yet I see it in the church all the time.

The question is, Do we want to play our personal favorites while our children and grandchildren find spiritual renewal elsewhere, or do we want to have our family together in the church? By instituting a dynamic worship style, we encourage multigenerational attendance. E. Stanley Ott says in *Twelve Dynamic Shifts for Transforming Your Church,* "In American culture today, huge shifts in expectations, lifestyles, and the understanding of truth are radically changing how people perceive the church and their very receptivity to the gospel." George Barna expresses a similar sentiment, saying, "Change is difficult but facilitates spiritual growth."[11] Rather than belaboring the age-old discussion of the church's inability to change, I would submit the vision of a preferred future of the church.

This future is broader than dynamic worship. It is the salvation, inclusion, and participation of family members and friends who currently are not active in the church, but could be if we were willing to deny ourselves, take up our crosses, and follow Jesus. Jesus did not care about having things his way. He prayed, "Not my will, but your will be done" (Luke 22:42). Jesus wanted things God's way, and God desires that all persons would be saved. The harsh truth is that in most cases the congregation refuses the faith change requested by God, and so, like the rich young ruler, turns away sorrowful because it cannot forsake its possessions. Our challenge is to change this sad commentary of the church.

As regards the worship components themselves, their delivery should be, as has been previously mentioned, in an upbeat tempo. When transitioning a worship service from the sedate to the dynamic, the congregation must evolve from being spectators to becoming participants. The worship leader is the catalyst for encouraging the enthusiastic participation of the congregation in worship. The encouragement to clap with the upbeat tempo of the songs can become a standard worship practice.

The introduction of praise, or the leading and the liberating of the people in spontaneous, personal worship expressions, can become the staging point for divine intervention and dynamic worship. From a member's heartrending story of some recent experience of God's grace, to the physical expression of active and visible praise, to someone giving his or her life to Christ, dynamic worship occurs when authentic and unrehearsed spiritual intervention takes place. This is not to be quenched. It is to be hoped for and celebrated. In such cases, someone is getting the ministry he or she needs to deal with trials.

Of course, it is the worship leader's responsibility to be the steward of the progressive flow of the worship service. Just as the leader should not abuse the congregation by taking advantage of their presence to talk to much, so should one or two participants not be allowed to abuse the congregation by usurping control of the worship, at least on a regular basis, and thereby removing the decency and order of worship. The worship must be structured enough to afford a sense of the divine stability and the unchanging aspect of God, while being free of the law of rigidity that stifles more than nurtures the spiritual life of the worshipers. An important responsibility of the worship leader is to maintain a progressive flow of worship while embracing the presence of the Holy Spirit. The worship should be dynamic while also proceeding through its order in a timely fashion.

When there is an older, more traditional style of worship, I recommend that praise be introduced to the worship in a deliberate and strategic manner. "It takes time to imbed an idea into the life of a congregation. Don't rush implementing ideas."[12] When I first arrived at DuPage and began to incorporate praise in worship, I began with a regular moment of hand-clapping and praise in the middle of the worship, just before our announcements. As time passed, whenever the choir would sing and the people were visibly moved by the selection, I would prolong the praise and applause and even incite more of it.

As the months proceeded, sometimes after the sermon, on Sundays when the Lord had particularly blessed the Word with power, the Spirit would be high with the atmosphere filled with electricity. At these times, I would precede the invitation to Christian discipleship with prolonged, extended, and encouraged praise. I gradually seized every opportunity to ignite the worship with the dynamism of fervent praise.[13] Every now and then, as the Spirit would lead me, I would call for a testimony or a special altar call. The blessings that occurred through these instances of obedience are too great and numerous to detail. I was always affirmed in this direction with some spiritual victory.

In subsequent years, as I became comfortable following the Spirit, I would even spontaneously change the order of worship completely once or twice a year. The emphasis here is to gradually effect change. I wanted to attract and keep the new generation, but I wanted also to keep the older generation, who had been faithful over the years. Rapid change can turn off longstanding members of the church. There is a delicate balance between introducing new worship forms and not eliminating familiar worship practices that must be maintained in transitioning a church's style of worship. The worship leader must struggle with the tension between these two practices but also be deliberate in progressively facilitating the transition of the worship style.

The worship at DuPage has evolved so that now the intervention of the Holy Spirit, as evidenced by dynamic and spontaneous praise, testimony, or some other intervention can occur at any point during worship. Sometimes in the very beginning of the service, as the call to worship is being given, I encourage the people in praise. The Holy Spirit catches fire so that several other worship components have to be deleted because the time of praise has consumed the time allotted for liturgy, hymn singing, or announcements. Every now and then the choir sings so high and hot on their first selection, a "spiritual fire" is set to the praise that follows. When the praise settles, *I will preach right there!* Then I will offer the invitation, receive the offering, and go home. The phone lines buzz so much after church that the next Sunday the church is full of excited people who are anticipating something unexpected. Then I return to the regular order and wait on the Spirit rather than repeating under my own direction. Worship and praise should be authentic and not manufactured.[14] Whenever the Spirit arrives, that's when I let God have God's way.

The worship should grow into being upbeat, enthusiastic, and participatory on the part of the congregation. I could say a lot here about the worship leader challenging himself or herself to becoming more dynamic. This is a spiritual growth challenge. Liturgy and readings must be delivered with vibrancy and creativity. Hymns and songs must be led with all the gusto of enthusiastic direction. You can't just stand still behind the pulpit. You can't sit on the pulpit with condescending dignity throughout the worship and expect the congregation to participate with enthusiasm. Leadership, in God's Realm, is best done by way of example. The worship leader must loosen up in order to encourage the worship team and the congregation in their own liberated praise. Growth leadership must be a team effort under the orchestrated leadership of the pastor.[15]

To a great extent music leads the way in worship. It is of such great importance that it is secondary only to the proclamation of the Word. Providing for music that will accommodate worship is a worthy investment of the church because good music helps create quality worship and "quality worship attracts people."[16] Worship that is dynamic has always depended a great deal on good music, and contemporary worship is no exception. I have stated that in a practical sense dynamic worship is worship that has an upbeat tempo.

"Upbeat" does not mean "upvolume." The instruments are not going to heaven. Only the people who are praying right are going to heaven. The drums are not damned instruments. The drummer does not have to beat the hell out of them. The music is a worship accompaniment. If the singing voices cannot be heard, then the music is too loud. If you cannot share a word with the person next to you and be heard, then the music is too loud. So the music has to be revved up in tempo, but it also has to balance its upbeat tempo with a volume that is still an accompaniment. When this occurs, then music is at its best in supporting dynamic worship. Let's move now from the pace of worship to the flow of worship.

Worship Flow

Therefore, since we are receiving a Realm that cannot be shaken, let us give thanks, by which we offer to God an acceptable worship with reverence and awe. — HEBREWS 12:28

For worship to be dynamic its flow must be continuous and its components must move fluidly from one to another. Dead space quenches the spirit in worship. When we disconnect each worship component with the dead or empty space of waiting for the next person to get to the rostrum, waiting for the choir to get ready to sing their selection, waiting for a congregant to walk to the announcement podium, waiting for church officers or ushers to position themselves for the offering, and so on, then we are interrupting the worship and preventing if from reaching its full dynamic potential. Worship should flow like cream poured smoothly and steadily from a pitcher until the pitcher is empty. Worship should be a continuation of components knitted together so smoothly that the worship itself becomes one component and not the whole of many components. Let's look at a model of worship that exemplifies this concept.

Different churches begin worship in different ways. Some begin with an instrumental prelude, some with choral singing, some with a worship leader's pronouncement, etc. However worship is begun, it moves from one component to the next until it reaches its conclusion. One thing that can help the worship flow smoothly is continuous music. Soft background music playing during all the speaking parts and during the transitions helps maintain a flow of connectedness. At DuPage the musicians are instructed that music should be continuous throughout worship except when visitors are being introduced and after the sermon has begun. At all other times there should be some music playing. The style, volume, and tempo of the music will be determined by what is happening in the worship, but music should be continuous throughout.

One historic disjunction in the flow of worship occurs right before choral selections. Historically, the music would stop and the choir director would take his or her place before the choir, straighten up the music on the music stand, look at the choir and then direct them

CHECKLIST FOR THE
OPTIMUM WORSHIP SETTING

☐ Evaluate and optimize church location

☐ Improve "curb" appeal (church's outside appearance)

☐ Attend to parking accommodations (parking ministry)

☐ Welcome worshipers at the door

☐ Assist worshipers with seating

☐ Catalyze dynamic worship! (Have church!)

☐ Encourage worshiper fellowship

---

to stand, look at the accompanist and nod, and then begin the selection. Sometimes this disjunction is even more pronounced when the director, musicians, or choir president have a brief discussion concerning the selection before it is begun. What is being suggested here is that whenever the time for the choral selection arrives during the worship, it is usually the same time at every service.

The director, the choir, and the congregation know when the choir is going to sing. Now, hopefully, the choir has rehearsed the previous week. They generally know what they are going to sing during worship. There should be no disjunctive break in the flow of the worship preceding choral selections or any of the other worship components. What must be impressed upon the musicians and the choir is that the Spirit is moving worship in a new and different way, and worship flow is a big part of this difference. When the time for the choral selection arrives, the musicians should immediately begin a prelude for the selection to be sung while the choir is being directed to stand and prepare to sing. Then they can be directed to join the ongoing music as they begin their selection. Any break in the flow of worship from the preceding worship component to the selection should be eliminated.

The music department sometimes can be as delicate to instruct as it is important to the worship. I recommend great care when dealing with the music department because musicians can be sensitive about their art. Preaching is also an art, but as I learned in seminary, as great an art as it is, art does not save people. Jesus saves! Presenting these recommendations in a deliberate but patient manner can offer an opportunity and a challenge toward spiritual growth and not a confrontation about style or control. As in all things administrative, the biblical mandate of "speaking the truth in love" is a perfect guide for the victory of God, and working with musicians and choirs is no exception. It's not the pastor's way, or the board's way, it is rather the Lord's leading. Remember, "whoever is slow to anger has great understanding" (Prov. 14:29).

When the time comes during worship for the choral selection, the musicians should immediately end the previous component's music by either beginning transitional music for the choir or going into the music of the coming selection. Immediately going into the music of the selection is the best way. This reduces the transitional time by introducing the selection and assists the director in getting the choir up to sing. With transitional music, there still could be prolonged preparation on the director's and choir's part. All of these suggestions require a further preparation of the worship music by the musicians and the choir. Being a part of the church's music ministry is more than rehearsing and singing selections.

Dynamic worship requires music that supports the worship in its entirety and not just at moments of choral performance. When music supports the worship in its entirety, an opportunity for the musicians and the choir to expand their worship consciousness is created. Where before there may have been some indifference to the other parts of the worship, there is now a dynamic enhancement of the entire worship. I have seen choirs and musicians who are not challenged in this way actually exhibit boredom with the service when they were not singing their selection. As the choir is usually positioned in front of the congregation, this spirit of uninterest can easily spread to the worshipers. In today's world, people generally have shorter attention spans and require greater stimulation to keep involved.[17] George Barna encourages the church's response to such cultural shifts in *Marketing the Church*, when he says, "Today,

organizational survival requires the ability to evaluate the environ-
ment and adapt one's style to keep pace with the change." In most
cases, musicians are paid employees of the church and not volunteers, so there can be a higher expectation of professionalism on
their part.

Ministers, officers, members, and even special guests who may participate in worship must also receive some preparation. Worshipers
must be trained in the experience of a continuous worship flow, and
this education must be persistent and vigorous.[18] When there are several worship participants moving to the podium, the time waiting
for each to arrive should be minimal. The next speaker should be
ready to take the place of the current speaker. Persons who are making announcements should be instructed to sit in the front of the
sanctuary.

When the congregation has to wait for people to excuse themselves out of the pew and then to walk in a grand processional to
the podium to begin speaking, this only creates an empty space
in worship. Special guest speakers, particularly those who are not
preaching, must be clearly instructed concerning the worship priorities so that they will be expedient in their presentations. These
suggestions, like many others in this book, may be great challenges
for many congregations. The churches that are used to doing things
the same way with the same people will have the toughest time. The
changes in worship that I am suggesting may affect the familiar and
identifying characteristics of the congregation.

The aspects of worship that endear the congregation to the church
may become vulnerable. I am convinced that when the pastor and
the church leadership can impress upon the congregation that these
recommendations bring the hope of new life for the church and get
a commitment in faith for their adoption, then there will be a statistically verifiable increase in attendance, participation, finances, and
spiritual growth. When the flow of worship becomes as great a priority as the individual worship components themselves, then the result
will be a worship that more greatly fulfills its own spiritual potential. Remember, "people are not made to enjoy our beautiful worship
services. Worship is given so God and the worshiper can commune
more deeply with each other."[19]

Timeliness of Worship

But as for me, my prayer is to you, O Lord.
At an acceptable time, O God,
in the abundance of your steadfast love, answer me.

— PSALM 69:13

I once had a guest speaker who, when witnessing the continuous flow and connectedness of our worship components, made the comment that everything was quick, quick, quick. When the time for the sermon arrived, his preliminary salutations and comments were concise, and then he said, "Let me move quickly into my sermon." I'm glad that the tone of our worship caused him to expedite his preliminary comments, which usually would have been prolonged. I have found that most preliminary comments are informative and interesting, even personally expressive and endearing to hear, but that in most cases they simply prolong the worship and are not spiritually edifying. As persons with a responsibility to lead worship, we must not only ask ourselves "What is worship?" we must also ask, "Who is worshiping?" Times and people have changed. As children, we used to say, "Either change with the times or get left behind." If the church is to keep from being left behind by those it is called to serve, then its worship and our understanding of worship must change. People no longer have the time to stay in worship all day. They simply are not going to do it. This again emphasizes the stewardship of worship flow. The great joy of worship is to tarry with the Spirit and this should never be circumvented. When the tarrying has been fulfilled, however, the worship must proceed. I tell my staff ministers who often lead worship to "Praise the Lord and move on!" "Programs that last for hours on end will lose people quickly."[20] People will come to church several times a week for business meetings and ministry activities. They will attend several worships in a week. Even on Sunday, although afternoon programs are not as well attended as they were in former years, a good number will still come on certain occasions. But most of us will agree that these are the exceptions and not the rule.

Here we are speaking more of the faithful few rather than the majority of the members. Our modern day commuter, computer culture has forced the life schedules of people to shift from what they were years ago. God is Spirit, but God is also a practical God.[21] In determining service times and lengths, we must exercise wisdom. Pastors and worship leaders should be considerate of what is the best way to reach the people.[22] This is another delicate balance that must be maintained so that dynamic worship can occur. We must accept that worship itself must not only give glory to God, but it must also afford God's people the best opportunity to do so. It is not a compromise of faith for pastors and worship leaders to outline the order of worship so that it may occur in a timely fashion.

I don't believe that the vast numbers of persons who are candidates for salvation are going to regularly attend a church service that takes over two hours, especially if it is long because of poor planning and worship quality. Worship is important and should be led with diligence and deliberation. Persons who are to be saved should not have to prove their faith by suffering unprepared worship leaders and worship participants. Most long worships are not long because the Spirit is high. They are long because people are taking their time about everything they are doing.

The worship service should always begin on time. This encourages the congregation to appreciate the importance of worship. A timely worship builds anticipation by creating a sense of urgency for those who are attending. It also encourages them to be prompt in their arrival at church. They know that they will miss something by being late. If the worship is scheduled to begin at a certain time, I suggest starting at that time no matter who is present. If it is important for people to be present and they are noticeably late, they will either make the timeliness of their arrival more of a priority, or the importance of their presence will become greatly diminished.

The Holy Spirit is always a welcome intervention in worship. The work of the Holy Spirit should represent the only prolongation of an otherwise ordered service. Worship can accomplish much more spiritually when it is intentionally led and deliberately participated in. We should not involve the worship of Holy God with the official business of the church. There is not much in terms of the life of the church that I would suggest should be totally excluded from worship. A good number of persons will never see some aspects of church life unless they somehow evidence themselves in worship.

There is usually some appropriate way within the parameters that have been discussed to present almost everything that is going on in the church through some aspect of the worship. But I reiterate that church business should be omitted from the worship experience. I firmly believe that when official church business regularly appears in worship that it diminishes the Holy Spirit's capacity to minister to the people. When people become distracted with their personal opinions, some small group struggle, or some secular consideration that church business can so often suggest, then the spiritual focus of the gathering is interrupted by social, political, or economic considerations.

I am not suggesting that there be no venue for the business of the church, but worship is not that venue. "For everything there is a season, and a time for every matter under heaven" (Eccl. 3:1). Worship is about glorifying God and not for critiquing a board meeting vote. When people have to think about the business of the church, it engages their mental and emotional faculties in a way that is personally constricted and not spiritually liberated. Who wants to come to church on Sunday and deal with what in most cases has the potential to be worrisome at best and a mess at worst? Worship is the time of free ministry and is best kept unencumbered with the dull pettiness of church business.

To those who say that Sunday worship is the only time that they have the people together to discuss church business, I would respond that you are not having a true worship service that day. What you are having is a religious business meeting. In addition, you are not going to have as many people regularly coming to church as you otherwise could because people have enough to worry about without coming to worship to worry about church business. People today come to church on Sunday to meet God and to experience the presence of the divine. They do not come to meet the chairman of the church board and to deliberate on board business.

This argument for a pure worship is not to diminish the need for the church to conduct its business. Conducting the business of the church is a practical necessity of its corporate structure. It would be irresponsible for those persons who are the leadership of the church to neglect their obligation to exercise managerial stewardship in the business areas with which they have been entrusted. I am merely suggesting that the business of the church be conducted at a time other than the time designated for worship. I am putting forth a recommendation of how a church can reach its fullest spiritual potential in worship. Matthew 11:19b says, "Wisdom is vindicated by her deeds." A common saying is that the proof is in the pudding. If you have a sanctuary that is filled to overflowing for worship and you regularly discuss the business of the church at length during worship, then by all means keep doing so. If, however, you have a lot of empty seats during worship and are praying about how they might be filled and you regularly discuss church business, then this suggestion represents a viable option for increasing your attendance.

Of course, there are exceptions to every rule. Over the years, there may come a time when some particular church business that is of great importance demands an appropriate comment or reference during the worship service. But if the Sunday service regularly includes detailed and prolonged presentations concerning church business, then that church will simply not be a church whose worship is fully dynamic.

Finally, in terms of worship timeliness — and this affects worship flow also — I repeat an earlier statement that extemporaneous talking kills the Spirit. When, as worship leaders or participants, we engage in prolonged comments, particularly personal stories and reflections, we run the risk of abusing the congregation because they are a captive audience. We may even be unintentionally usurping the worship from the Holy Spirit.

Occasionally, when the Spirit leads, dynamic worship must allow and include personal testimony. But to regularly have personal meanderings on topics unrelated to the glory of God is not spiritually edifying and therefore not conducive to worship. Yes, worship is a communal gathering for fellowship and sharing, but worship is also regularly abused with long reflections on topics that are not conducive to worship. I believe that in order for worship to be effective it must be more pure than it has evolved to be in some settings. When people get in front of a crowd in any venue, they often forget how long they are speaking. It simply is not reverent to God or good stewardship of worship to prolong the worship for this reason. With few exceptions, the day for the Sunday pulpit to be a place of commentary through anything other than a prayer or sermon has past.

It will help any pastor or worship leader to remember that talking kills the spirit.

The Management of Worship

And since we have a great priest over the house of God, let us approach with a true heart in full assurance of faith, with our hearts sprinkled clean from an evil conscience and our bodies washed with pure water.

— HEBREWS 10:21–22

The suggestions in this chapter have been made for the purpose of guiding worship into a greater spiritual vibrancy. If you want your church to attract more people, have a higher Spirit, become more active with ministries, and gather more finances and other resources for Realm-building work, then I pray that these ideas be seriously considered. What may not be evident but which I must add is that whenever worship is called it must be managed. Like a board meeting, a project, or a group of workers, worship must be managed. Usually this is the pastor's job, with the help of a willing and supportive staff. This is a necessary responsibility for dynamic worship. From start to finish, someone must be observing and directing the worship. Someone has to make sure that the support staff is in place and that the worship begins on time. Someone has to make sure that the worship participants are moving in an intentional and expeditious fashion. Someone has to make sure that the music is on target. There is no way that all of the suggestions in this chapter can be fully implemented, nor that any worship can proceed dynamically, unless deliberate management is taking place. If the worship is not managed, then it can easily return to listless routine and lifeless song. In such cases it is not unusual for well-meaning but uncoordinated individuals to take charge. This results in a worship that is a disjunctive and confusing experience. A pattern of such experiences results in a church with a mediocre worship experience and "there is no reason we should put up with mediocrity, just because we are a charitable (i.e., volunteer and spiritual), organization."[23] Worship must be managed to facilitate both order and dynamism.

A VISION OF PERFECT WORSHIP
FOR DUPAGE AME CHURCH

1. PARKING ATTENDANTS
   Be prepared *every* Sunday to make full use of all four parking lot areas with a van shuttle regardless of attendance.

2. HOSPITALITY & USHERS
   Have prayer together as soon as two or three have arrived and be in place five minutes before service.

3. MINISTERS
   All ministers in the pastor's office five minutes before service.

4. MUSIC
   CD music playing in the sanctuary ten minutes before service until pastor stands at pulpit.

5. MUSICIANS
   In place when ministers enter pulpit (five minutes before service time).

6. CHOIRS (7:00 a.m. and 8:15 a.m. services)
   In loft as service is open.

7. CHOIRS (11:15 a.m. service)
   Choir at sanctuary door prepared for processional as service opens.

8. PROCESSIONAL
   Immediately as opening praise is ending without breaks or open spots.

9. SERVICE (11:15 a.m.)
   Doxology *immediately* as choir ends processional (no break).

10. SERVICE (11:15 a.m.)
    Opening hymn (music) introduction *immediately* upon Doxology ending (or as praise diminishes at 7:00 and 8:15 a.m. services).

11. INVOCATION MUSIC
    Begins *immediately* upon hymn ending (even as people are taking their seats).

12. CHORAL SELECTION MUSIC
    Begins *immediately* upon invocation response ending. (Choir stands even as selection intro music has begun.) Please be mindful of selection and lengths.

13. ANNOUNCEMENTS begin *immediately* after choral selection/praise ends.
    Congregation members making approved announcements should move to the front pews and use either podium. When called, the first announcer establishes protocol. The following announcer should simply state, "Protocol has been established." It is not necessary to acknowledge the pastors, ministers, etc., over and over again. Announcers are not introduced. They should introduce themselves. The second announcer should begin on the opposite podium as the first announcer ends or come to the same podium as the previous announcer is leaving. Cut out waiting time.

14. VISITORS

    Visitors are announced *immediately* after the last announcer finishes. They should state their name and whom they are visiting with only. Then each visitor should take his or her seat (with love and honor).

15. MUSIC

    "Sweet, Sweet Spirit" music begins *immediately* after the last visitor is acknowledged. (Even as minister is thanking visitors for their attendance)

16. MINISTERS

    Ministers' gathering in the pulpit with pastor during fellowship. All gatherings will end with prayer for the "preacher."

17. OFFERINGS

    Begins *immediately* after visitors' song. Minister must be at the podium waiting with officers of the day already standing at the altar. The ushers process as the minister directs the congregation to read stewardship emphasis. Officers of the Day offer prayer *immediately* after page 9 is read. Cue: "Are you a Tither, will you become one today?"

18. BAPTISMS

    When baptisms are performed, music begins *immediately* after fellowship, offering, or invitation, as directed by the pastor.

19. SERMONIC/OFFERING CHOIR SELECTION

    Choral selection should begin *immediately* upon officer of the day's Amen. Move to conclude selection when ushers process to altar for the second time.

20. SERMON

    The sermon begins *immediately* as ushers are recessing. Twenty minutes please, and limit protocol and other extemporaneous statements. Simply preach the Word.

21. INVITATIONAL HYMN

    Begins *immediately* after sermon, as sermon is ending, as preacher directs, or before preacher sits down when a guest is preaching.

22. NEW MEMBER INTRODUCTIONS

    Introductions begin *immediately* after invitation even if roll signing is not complete.

23. DOXOLOGY MUSIC

    Begins *immediately*, even if minister is not yet behind pulpit. "Praise God from Whom All Blessings Flow."

24. POSTLUDE MUSIC

    Musicians play for five minutes after benediction.

In Conclusion

Facilitating a spirit-filled worship is a labor of love, but it is still labor. It is still work. There are so many things that go into creating a dynamic worship experience that we could never address them all. We, however, would be remiss if we did not emphasize the personal spiritual preparation that is necessary for authentic worship to occur. Although worship is a God-centered activity, it may surprise you that "one third of the worshipers have never experienced God's presence."[24] In the following chapter that deals with personal spiritual growth, attention will be given to the primary and divine purpose of all church activity. The end result is not simply for us to have churches that are full of more people who are giving more money. Those are simply forms of evidence that may indicate that we are reaching our divine purpose.

The divine purpose of the Christian faith is for Christians to become like Jesus. More specifically, the church should facilitate its members in spiritual growth so that their lives exemplify the life of Jesus. The divine goal of the Christian faith is not attained by the amount of money we give or the tenure of our service. The divine goal of the Christian faith is for us to become spiritually mature, and quite simply, spiritual maturity is being like Christ. The more like Christ we are, the more spiritually mature we are. When the worship of Holy God has occurred, we should leave with more than a good feeling. We should leave empowered and emboldened to reach toward this high calling.

EIGHT

Personal and Congregational Spiritual Growth

But grow in the grace and knowledge of our Lord and Savior Jesus Christ. To him be the glory, both now and to the day of eternity. Amen.
— 2 PETER 3:18

THROUGH MUCH PRAYER AND SUPPLICATION, the ministry of DuPage was guided in growth that is statistically verifiable. The evaluating qualifiers are an increase in both the number of members and the amount of tithes and offerings. To achieve these goals, several other dynamic and growing ministries were used as models for our ministry, and we adapted ourselves to those principles and practices that were conducive to our growth. We observed these ministries and learned from them, appropriating these lessons into the faith expressions of our church. The goal was to develop our ministry so that it would be attractive to persons who were seeking a church home. The primary attractions of DuPage were always in our worship of the Lord and our fellowship with each other, but the inspiration our members received to develop their own faith has been the sustaining factor. Proverbs 11:14 says, "In an abundance of counselors there is safety."

As a congregation we were exposed to the most dynamic pastors and congregations in our sphere of fellowship. When I could no longer find models in my immediate geographical area, I looked beyond the local landscape in order to learn from the wisdom and practices of others. I attended ministry conferences and workshops and brought back fresh ideas, applying those that were best suited to our mission and ministry. The Lord blessed us with dynamic growth as we labored in these Realm building efforts.

On a sunny Easter Sunday morning several years ago, for the first time our attendance was more than one thousand persons worshiping at DuPage. This should have been a day of great joy and affirmation for me, but quite interestingly, on that day a sort of pall fell over my countenance. This was most curious when you consider that each and every week it had been my job to stir up the energy in almost everyone else. I take great joy in being the initiator of the spiritual fervor around me in fellowship and worship. Ironically, on that particular Sunday the tables turned. Everyone else was jubilant. The staff ministers were overflowing with the joys of salvation and all who were present were celebrating the victory of the resurrection. But for some strange reason, I was subdued and almost saddened in my spirit.

The burden upon my spirit steadily increased as I persevered through our first two services and then through the church school hour. This spiritual weight became so heavy that as we began the third and final service of the day, I excused myself from the pulpit and retired to a private room adjoining the pulpit so that I could pray. Alone there, with the worship continuing outside, tears filled my eyes. In this secluded moment, I inquired of God concerning this spirit that was upon me. I remember my petition, "Lord, this is a day that I have labored and longed for. The spirit is high and the church has been filled to overflowing and yet, instead of celebration, my soul is troubled within me. We have finally broken the four digit mark and seen over one thousand people, and yet I am sad. How can this be?"

God responded clearly, "Is that what this is all about for you? How many people you see on Sunday morning? Is that all there is?" Under that conviction, I wept tears of both sorrow and joy. Sorrow because I realized how easily the focus of Christianity, the saving of souls, and the improvement of lives is lost in the secularism of statistical analysis. Joy because I realized that for me this was a kairos moment, an epiphany of revelation and true, pure personal spiritual growth. In a pivotal moment of ministry, divine purpose had again been revealed to me and it was "life, and life abundantly." Let me be clear in the point that I am making. It is not that ministries should emphasize quality over quantity. Both have their place in the substance and evidence of faithful ministry. The debate of quality versus quantity is not what is being argued here. What is being emphasized is the spiritual beauty of an episode of personal spiritual growth.

I believe that the foundation of every saved person is a conversion experience. Somewhere on the path of life, God's presence manifests itself clearly to that person, and when that person accepts Jesus Christ as Lord and Savior, he or she is saved. Consequently, each saved life must be built through personal spiritual growth. Just as continuing education is crucial to the effective relevance of any ongoing pursuit, personal spiritual growth must also continue in the pursuit of holiness. Many churches lose the emphasis of personal spiritual growth in the push for the corporate spiritual growth of the church body through its programs, projects, and other ministerial activities. Yet, "knowing God does not come through a program or a method. It is a relationship with a person. God reveals his will, then invites you to join him where he is already at work."[1]

Sanctification may be defined as "the process of being made perfect through the Holy Spirit."[2] God is always present to instruct us in and inspire us toward personal spiritual improvement. A sanctified life is a life that shows continued progress in increasing the priorities of God and decreasing the priorities of the world and the flesh.[3] A continued series of kairos moments, moments that reveal and affirm the reality of God working in our lives, is to be desired for the benefit of our spiritual maturity and our goal of becoming like Christ. Quite often these moments come in the midst of the great challenges of our lives, when we find our souls most troubled.[4] Allow me to share another story that illustrates this point.

A Crisis of Belief

Satan has desired to sift all of you like wheat.
— LUKE 22:31

After the new worship facility for DuPage was completed, we experienced a time of explosive growth. We had returned to a single Sunday morning worship service schedule, but our growth required an immediate consideration of returning to two Sunday morning services.

Being naïve, I thought that this was a thing the entire congregation would be happy about. I quickly discovered, however, that there were more members who were excited about the new building, and the nicer accommodations, than were excited about ongoing spiritual growth and Realm building opportunities.

My discovery presented administrative challenges for leading the congregation in this needed expansion of our worship opportunities. As the pastor, I felt that this was my responsibility. As it turned out, it was also a perfect opportunity for God to seize this season of my ministry for the purpose of challenging my own personal spiritual growth. God used this challenge to bring about dynamic and sure growth in my personal faith walk. In order to do this, a personal change had to occur.

In initiating the two service worship schedule, I faced opposition from some of the church officers. Arguments such as "We don't want to be divided," "We can't afford a two service budget," and "It's too complicated to keep up with" — along with a chorus of other objections — presented a formidable roadblock. Although I understood most of their rationale, I knew that the Lord was leading me to pursue this direction. This was the divine path for our church, but to boldly take a stance and to move forward, regardless of the sentiments around me, was not comfortable for me. I have a non-confrontational personality. In group dynamics and relational interaction, I operate as a consensus builder and a unifier. Obeying God through such confrontation had not previously been so unavoidably required of me.

I made the mistake of taking the opposition from the board as a personal affront. I forgot the words of the Apostle Paul in Ephesians 6:12: "For our struggle is not against enemies of blood and flesh, but against the rulers, against the authorities, against the cosmic powers of this present darkness, against the spiritual forces of evil in the heavenly places." I now understand that the majority of the board members who were in opposition were not opposing me personally, and they certainly were not overtly rebelling against God. I prayed to the Lord and God clearly answered me, saying, "I know who you are because I made you. Now decide. Either you will be with the people, or you will be with me." God has a way of speaking to everyone who listens, and it was settled for me in the moment of God's response. The prospect of walking without God in my life and ministry was too frightening a prospect to consider. At the next scheduled meeting, I shared my prayers with the board, and subsequently with the church body. I informed them that we were going to a two Sunday morning worship service schedule, and I set the starting date for those services.

Unfortunately, I didn't set the best starting date. I started the two services at the worst possible time, which was the month of June when the members began to go on their summer vacations. Instead of having one well-attended service we now had two services with low attendance. If I had read Charles Arn's *How to Start a New Service,* which I hadn't at that time, I never would have chosen that date. That summer was a catastrophe for me. I carried the weight of having seemingly made what was clearly a bad decision. The weight of the burden of that bad decision increased every Sunday. The congregation was uneasy in its spirit and the officers were greatly disturbed. Whispers about the stagnation of DuPage's near flawless growth progression were to me like deafening shouts. The rumor mill began to work, gossip was spreading, and it was even mentioned that the power of my preaching had diminished. It wasn't the best of times.

By mid-August the burden became too much for me. I told Rev. Lana that I thought the church should go back to one Sunday service. I thank God for a good wife and partner in ministry. She reminded me that such an action would not represent our faith in God's promises. We also discussed how my leadership equity, that had taken so many years to build, would be highly compromised if I did this. God's vision should never be abandoned in a moment of crisis. This was my lesson to learn. Sometimes we think we have learned a lesson, but rational knowledge and practical experience are two different things. As we continue in ministry, our knowledge as well as our faith will be tested and re-tested to prove its viability.[5] Bishop Philip R. Cousin Sr., my bishop at the time of this writing, has another way of saying this: "Don't ever think you are so slick that you can't take another greasing."

A Truth about Obedience

When the Spirit of truth comes, he will guide you into all truth.
— JOHN 16:13A

If the foundations are destroyed, what can the righteous do?
— PSALM 11:3

I was in a spiritual crisis. My wife often says, "All flesh will cry out under suffering." I again went into fervent prayer with God, and it was there that my soul received cause for rejoicing. God told me quite plainly, "Jimmy, if the whole thing falls apart, you still will have been faithful!" In that moment of stress, what a wonderful revelation and liberation this was for me! The victory was not in my ministerial comfort or success; it was in my Christian faith! This is an important lesson for all Christians in the mega-church and prosperity culture of our time. Secular success and faith victory are not necessarily the same. "Successful leaders serve the bottom line, faithful leaders serve God."[6]

My soul was set free of bondage. I began preaching with joy and walking in peace once again. When the summer ended, the Lord rewarded my faithfulness. By the end of September both services had filled to near capacity. Great days of victory and vindication had arrived, but this is not what I am emphasizing. The point I am making is that this was a season of growth in my life as well as in the life of the church. There were clear, culminating kairos moments of genuine personal spiritual growth for all of us. God affirmed and increased our faith through intervention, instruction, and inspiration. The victory is not that the program was successful or that I was right. The victory is that my relationship with God was strengthened.

The Problem with Being Right

There is only one who is good.
— MATTHEW 19:17B

One pervasive problem we must guard against in church ministry is the penchant to be right while others are wrong. Most often, as regards some issue of administrative or ministerial concern, the pastor ends up being right, or an officer ends up being right, but then they are right all by themselves, because the people around them have departed. I often say, "Why would I want to be right and then be all by myself, when I can prayerfully consider the views of others and have a crowd?" God wants ministries to flourish with genuine personal spiritual growth. God is well able to prove what is right whenever that is necessary. The integrity of any Christian walk must be a continuing series of episodes like those just previously presented. This is the necessary continuing education of any Christian's faith walk. It is one process of sanctification. God's desire for the perfection of God's people is repeated throughout the scriptures. It begins and continues with the humility, appreciation, and obedience generated by being faithful through personal struggles and challenges. It ends with the blessings of God that result from God's sure and eternal promises. The more such encounters we have, the more we grow in God and God grows in us.

Spiritual Practice makes Spiritual Perfection

Be perfect, therefore, as your heavenly Father is perfect.
— MATTHEW 5:48

Jesus called his followers to become disciples. You cannot be a disciple without practicing discipline. Discipline is a necessary element of authentic and genuine personal and corporate spiritual growth. In *Good to Great*, Jim Collins says "The transformation process of build up to break through has three stages: disciplined people, disciplined thought, and disciplined action."

Discipline implies a deliberate way of being. This may be why the followers of Christ were initially referred to as those who were in "the way," or "the way of regularly being like Jesus." So much of God's Realm and creation is established with a system of regularity and dependability. Once God establishes a thing, it is fixed. The sun rises the way God ordained it. The seasons change as God ordained them. The cycle of life continues as God ordained it. Likewise, the rewards

SPIRITUAL PRACTICE MAKES SPIRITUAL PERFECTION

Daily Prayer

- ☦ Private (in your home or where the spirit leads)
- ☦ Public (at church, restaurants, family gatherings)

Bible Study

- ☦ Private (daily, in your home or where the spirit leads)
- ☦ Public (at Sunday Church School or other group settings; Wednesday Bible Study, 7:15 p.m.)

Periodic Fasting

- ☦ Private (as God leads you)
- ☦ Public (with the church body every Wednesday, in the way God leads you)

Regular Worship

- ☦ Public (EVERY SUNDAY)
- ☦ Private (in your home on a regular basis or for special occasions)

Mission

- ☦ Active participation in Christian outreach ministry (using the gifts God gave you, working where God places you)

Tithing

- ☦ 10 percent of the first fruits belong to GOD. Don't forget the stewardship of time and talent.

If my people, who are called by my name,
will humble themselves and pray
and seek my face and turn from their wicked ways,
then will I hear from heaven and will forgive their sin
and will heal their land.
2 Chronicles 7:14

of faith are certain when the spiritual disciplines are regularly practiced. I believe that the basic spiritual disciplines in the order of their priority are: daily prayer, daily Bible study, weekly worship, regular Realm building participation, tithing, and fasting. Any one of these disciplines accesses God's response of blessing through the "divine DNA" of regularity and dependability, and tithing is a perfect example. Its basis is in obedience. Its righteousness is in equity. Its spirit is in thanksgiving. Its hope is in expectation. Its practice, however, is in regularity and dependability. Tithing establishes a resource for God's work that can be counted on, and this heavenly reciprocity is true for all spiritual practices. Our consistent exercise of spiritual practices is the evidence of our faithfulness, and spiritual disciplines are essential for the growth and maturity of any Christian.[7]

In terms of priority, cultivating our relationship with God is rooted and grounded in the discipline of personal devotions. Daily prayer maintains our communion with God and daily Bible study provides us with information about God's will for our lives. These are essential above all others in positioning our souls for the kairos moments that become the clear markers of our spiritual growth.

All persons of faith would agree that a discipline of personal devotions is a priority for spiritual health, growth, and well-being. Most, however, confess that in their personal devotions they are not as disciplined as they feel that the Lord would have them to be. We live lives that are so busy that when we awaken we are often already late for the day's activities. In *Staff Your Church for Growth*, Gary McIntosh says, "The lifestyle of most people today reduces their time for spiritual growth." Maintaining spiritual discipline is a lifestyle choice that requires decision, determination, and dedication. Joshua 24:15a says, "Choose this day whom you will serve," and this is our constant faith challenge.

We revel in our ability to multitask, and society encourages and rewards this pressured existence. Our lives are so complex that the consistency of unforeseen interruptions can cause our Christian disciplines to be disjunctive and irregular. Our hastened life pace continually urges us beyond the fullness of our present experience. We are constantly overcoming our past and contemplating the future while we miss being in the here and now.[8]

My first encouragement in establishing spiritual discipline is to "make quiet time." Rick Warren mentions this in *The Purpose-Driven Church* as a part of a spiritual maturity covenant. Our God is a jealous God. God wants our attention and a clear demonstration of our professed love and faith. Henry Blackaby shares in *Experiencing God*, "A love relationship with God requires a demonstration of obedience." In today's modern world, the greatest enemy of quiet time with God is our attachment to technological instruments. If we are to prioritize spending time with God, we must relinquish our fixation on the technologies around us and put them in the proper place of being tools and not companions. The ever present gadgets of today's culture are objects of work or recreation, but they are not friends.

Martin Luther King Jr. is quoted as saying, "The internal is the realm of the Spirit. The external is that complex of devices. Our problem today is that we have allowed the internal to become lost to the external."[9] From beginning to end, each day is cluttered with a dependency on technology. An alarm clock awakens us and electronic music lulls us into sleep. Computers and video games are trancelike preoccupations. Even when there is no desirable television show to watch, we mindlessly press our remote control buttons, surfing the airwaves from channel to channel. In order to refocus our attention on the spiritual we must break this near addiction of technological dependency.

The faith challenge is to consciously be intentional about ensuring that time is made available for spiritual reflection. When you first awaken from sleep and as your day proceeds, think twice before you turn on any instrument. You could be robbing God and yourself of some quiet time together. This is not to suggest an abdication from the systems of modern-day communication. I praise God for the progress of science and technology. In their proper place they are indispensable to the progressive development of people everywhere. But if our present and future generations are losing their spiritual edge, a primary reason is our constant interaction with instruments as a substitute for our relationships with God and with each other. Psalm 46:10 says, "Be still, and know that I am God!" Exodus 14:13 says, "Stand firm, and see the deliverance that the Lord will accomplish for you today." Psalm 23:2 says, "He leads me beside still waters; he restores my soul." Stillness allows us to focus on God, give God attention, and receive attention from God in a most personal way. Stillness requires quiet time and a quiet spirit.[10]

Preserving quiet time for God is a spiritual discipline, and like any other discipline it is not an overnight or onetime effort. It is a long-term commitment whose benefits are revealed over the long haul. Therefore, if you have an interruption in your discipline, which is inevitable, don't let the interruption be the end of the discipline. For instance, if you are on a diet and you momentarily go off your diet and eat your favorite dessert, that should not be the end of your diet. Enjoy your dessert, but the next day, get back on your diet. Don't go out and eat three seven-course meals because you momentarily went off your diet. If you get back on your diet you will not have done much damage at all. It's the same with physical exercise. If you are exercising every day and something happens so that you miss your exercise, don't give up on your exercise regimen. Instead, pick it back up the next day and you will not have done much damage.

The same principle applies to your spiritual discipline. You may miss some days of reading the Bible. You may have an interruption in your attendance at Bible study. But don't just leave your Bible to sit and gather dust. Pick it up the next time you pass it and begin your study again. Your prayer life may wane from time to time. Don't just forget how the floor feels when you are kneeling in prayer. Just stop yourself the next time the Spirit touches you and have a little talk with Jesus. The joy of the Lord will return and it will be your strength in maintaining the discipline. Making a daily space for quiet time with God is the first step in establishing a firm foundation for healthy spiritual growth. This is primary instruction for creating a culture of authentic spiritual growth in a church and must be continuously revisited with the congregation.

The Church as Spiritual Growth Facilitator

My house shall be a house of prayer.
— LUKE 19:46

A primary purpose of the church is to spread the Christian faith for the saving of souls. The primary purpose of this book is to facilitate statistically quantifiable church growth. The goal is to help your church have a larger number of worshipers in attendance and an increase in tithes and offerings. Yet, "any church growth strategy that is geared to increasing the number of people without emphasizing the necessity of commitment to Jesus Christ is working in opposition to scriptural command."[11] The church has a universal and cross-generational responsibility to fulfill its divine purpose of preserving the Christian faith for the salvation of souls. In order to accomplish this, biblical instruction and the encouragement to embrace it are fundamental. When people live out the teaching of Christ, their faithful obedience brings them into fellowship with Christ through the Holy Spirit.

It is interesting then that statistically only one-third of all Christian worshipers have actually experienced the authentic presence of the Holy Spirit.[12] This realization puts the effectiveness of the church as a transformative agent in the lives of its members under scrutiny. If we look at the social impact of the church in comparison with the many ills of society, the effectiveness of the church as a transformative agent is also subject to scrutiny. It is not sacrilegious for us to challenge the church's spiritual productivity. Evaluation is an accepted process of accountability and improvement. Our goal is to assess the church's methods in order to increase its effectiveness in spreading the gospel and in transforming society. As Laurie Beth Jones says in *Jesus, CEO*, "Accountability has nothing to do with blame. It has everything to do with individual and corporate growth." Jesus prayed, "Your kingdom come, your will be done, on earth as it is in heaven" (Matt. 6:10). The phrase "as it is in heaven" sets up a process of accountability and evaluation through comparison.

The Holy Spirit is the contemporary presence of God. The Holy Spirit is God with us today. In order to have spiritual power to affect present-day situations we must know God and be in right relationship with God through the Holy Spirit. What is the church doing to facilitate the knowledge of, and a relationship with, God the Holy Spirit? Does our language distinguish the personhood of God? God the Holy Spirit is a person, and how we address a person is fundamental to our relationship with him or her. Jesus knew this and always began his prayers to God as Father or "Our Father." This indicates the personhood of God.

I often have heard the Holy Spirit referred to as "it." The use of a personal pronoun in referencing people is a basic display of respect for who they are. Referencing the Holy Spirit as "it" presents God as an impersonal, material object. If one of your family members was referred to as an "it," that would be an insult to you and your family. We must reorient our thinking to acknowledge the Holy Spirit as a person. Church liturgies affirm this theological proposition, saying, "God in three *persons*, blessed trinity." When we talk about the Holy Spirit, we are dealing with a person of God and not an object of God's creation. When church members can reorient their frame of reference in this way, that reorientation advances a spiritual perspective that enhances their personal devotions and facilitates spiritual growth.

If the church is a developmental agent facilitating our knowledge of God the Holy Spirit, then the priorities and practices of the church must reflect that purpose. Does the church increase our knowledge of the Holy Spirit? Does the church guide us in cultivating a relationship with God the Holy Spirit? Is the church an institution of spiritual education and practice? And, more specifically, is it more of a social, political, and economic organization than it is a spiritual institution? As a transformative agent, the church must explore these inquiries.

Every ministry, program, and activity in the church should afford an opportunity for affirmative spiritual growth, and there should be an intensive, specific spiritual growth component as a part of each group's function. Knowing and experiencing God does not come through social, political, or economic priorities. Knowing and experiencing God comes through cultivating a personal relationship with God through the practice of spiritual disciplines. If the church has relegated church membership to a calendar of social programs, political agendas, and economic priorities, then the church has missed its calling. It has allowed secondary considerations to interfere with its primary purpose to be a transformative agent in society and in the lives of its members. In such cases, human effort and intellect become the guiding force and the dysfunction of this unfortunate condition soon becomes evident. The church becomes decreasingly able to maintain itself, let alone preserve, maintain, and forward the Christian faith.

The cultural response to the church's continuance in this direction is shared in George Barna's *The Frog in the Kettle:* "Our choice of a religious system will be based on that system's ability to satisfy our own personal needs and desires. Religion becomes less of a corporate experience and more of a self-fulfilling process. The local church will have to earn its place in people's hearts. Institutional loyalty, the presumption of their credibility, and altruistic support of them will largely disappear."[13] Perhaps this is what Paul was referring to in 2 Timothy 4:3, saying, "For the time is coming when people will not put up with sound doctrine, but having itching ears, they will accumulate for themselves teachers to suit their own desires." Many Christian leaders, members, and congregations accept their declining circumstance in order to preserve an outdated rationale. The number of souls lost and lives unchanged in the wake of this obstinacy is unconscionable. What the church needs is a radical reorientation of its faith in God through prioritizing the practice of spiritual disciplines. The spiritual development of the congregation can no longer be relegated to the midweek prayer meeting and Bible study that the majority of the church members do not attend. The church's social, fellowshiping attributes should be maintained; however its political, institutional aspects and its economic practices and theologies must be revised. We must be reminded that in the end, all that matters is Jesus.[14]

Spiritual Disciplines

These Jews were more receptive than those in Thessalonica, for they welcomed the message very eagerly and examined the scriptures every day to see whether these things were so.   — ACTS 17:11

One of the greatest myths of the Christian faith is that church members regularly practice spiritual disciplines. I was watching one of the most renowned Bible teachers on his telecast years ago. This is a man whose whole calling and ministry are based on teaching the sound and unadulterated doctrines of the Bible. He is the pastor of a mega-church. As I watched him teaching the lesson for the week, he asked everyone in the congregation who had read that week's lesson to raise their hands. In that congregation of thousands, a sparse few individuals raised their hands. The minister was so taken aback that he forsook his teaching and went to preaching for the rest of the program. It occurred to me that if people were not reading their Bibles in that great ministry based on Bible teaching, then what was the level of spiritual discipline in churches based on preaching, mission work, or other Christian ministries?

Most faithful Christians, though believing and trusting in God, are not reading the Bible with diligence and discipline. This indicates a diminished spiritual capacity in our prayer life and in the practice of our faith. Ministry leaders must never take for granted that the souls under their care are doing what they are being asked to do. I am not suggesting that tests and examinations be administered, although these may be effective and even enjoyable as a part of certain studies. I am suggesting that a continuous encouragement and a supportive structure that facilitates spiritual nurturance, through the practice of spiritual disciplines, be a regular, intentional responsibility of Christian leadership.

Given the sociopolitical involvements and priorities of the church, the question for each church leader is, Do you provide as many opportunities for the spiritual disciplines as you do for fellowshiping programs? Do you spend as much time preparing, organizing, and promoting opportunities for purely spiritual growth as you do for administration? Do you maintain a balance between promoting spiritual disciplines and effecting organizational concerns? Are the processes and methods of ministry that you use practical and feasible tools with which to provide holistic ministry to your congregation? How do we ensure that the doctrines we teach are sound and therefore spiritually healthy? There is a convicting and indicting question that probably does not apply to anyone reading this book but I will present it anyway. Is your evaluation of victorious ministry based in the triune God, the Holy Scriptures, and your personal conversion experience, or is it based in peer pressure, human reason, and contemporary statistical comparisons?

This book is primarily written to cultivate practical applications of Christian theology to improve administration in the local church. My basic theological premise and ministry guide has always been that "spirituality must meet practicality." In *The Five-Star Church*, Toler Nelson says, "A five-star church must always be centered on Jesus Christ and complemented with a pragmatic freedom within ministry."[15] My emphasis has always been that a practical application of spiritual imperatives is fundamental to ministerial success. To deny such practical applications is to deny the very Christ event itself. After all, "God is Spirit" (John 4:24), and yet "the Word became flesh and lived among us" (John 1:14). As regards ministry, we must find a way to appropriate the spiritual calling and direction from God in a way that can be effectively applied for the benefit of the church and the edification of God's people.

The reverse is also true. We cannot be so practical in the practice of Christian ministry as to neglect the spiritual essence that distinguishes the ministry from secular society. "Do not be conformed to this world, but be transformed by the renewing of your mind, so that you may discern what is the will of God, what is good and acceptable and perfect" (Rom. 12:2). Maintaining a balance between spiritual imperatives and practical applications allows us to affect and transform the society around us rather than being affected and transformed by society. With these considerations, our perspective on ministry can move from the ambition for secular success to the aspiration for faith victories.

In Conclusion

When a dialogue on the spiritual context of administrative practices is created, it provides encouragement for the challenge of joining theology with the operation of the church. Congregational and personal spiritual growth is a wonderful thing to behold. To witness persons growing out of their programmatic or personal views of church administration and evolving into a practical awareness of spiritual priorities is a worthy goal of church leadership. I believe that there is no practical need for an individual or for a church that God will not provide when that individual or church puts as much time into becoming spiritual as they do to developing and implementing programs. Attending and participating in church board meetings requires a lot of time and energy. When the church leaders meet in the administrative boards less and attend Bible study and other such activities more, an increased attendance in worship and offerings will result. This is not to forsake what has been presented in the previous chapters. It is rather to challenge the leadership in establishing a balance between rational and spiritual involvements, and specifically to tip the scales toward spiritual involvements in order to establish a proper balance. The reorientation toward spiritual priorities for the church membership will result in a statistical increase in quantifiable areas, as well as the victorious ministry of transformed lives.

There is one other feature of spiritual growth that is a primary distinction and that is its authenticity. When does spiritual growth actually take place and what is the evidence of genuine spiritual growth? A good answer is, "The spiritual marks of an effective church are changed lives."[16] If the goal of church membership is to become more like Christ, then how can we tell when this is occurring? Let me relay a family story about my father's ministerial calling that may provide a context for evaluating the authenticity of spiritual growth.

My father, the late Rev. Dr. Roy L. Miller, was raised on a farm in South Carolina. His parents were hard-working Christian people who were regular supporters and leaders in their church. My grandfather, Oscar Miller, was an active layman in the church and renowned in that area as an industrious worker and shrewd businessman. As a result of progressive decisions and much labor, he had success in his farming and increased his landholdings. He was a recognized layperson in the church, revered by ministers and bishops alike. Although he was a good church person, however, my grandfather was suspicious of ministers. I think he felt that most preachers were not the best Christian role models, and he did not hold the prospects of making a decent living through the ministry in high regard. He definitely did not like the way that most of the ministers he knew seemed to beg for their living. Maybe this is more of a critique on how the church has cared for its ministers than of the ministers themselves.

When my father received his call to the Christian ministry on Mother's Day in 1934, it was a day of mixed emotions for him. On the one hand, his soul was filled with the joy of the heavenly calling. On the other hand, he wondered how he would break the news to his father. He knew his father hoped that he would become successful in corporate business or in some other such profession. He knew that his father did not want him to beg for a living, even if it was in Jesus' name. He knew he faced the possibility of disapproval and disappointment from his father.

Late that Sunday, when dinner was over and the household was busy with its Sunday afternoon occupations, my dad walked with his dad out into the pastures surrounding the house and gingerly broke the news to him. My father relayed my grandfather's response in this manner. He said that as he stood there filled with anticipation and anxiety, his father looked off into the distance for a long moment as he pondered his son's revelation. Then, quite suddenly, he turned, looked him in the eyes, and said, "Well, if you are going to be a preacher, then be a real one." In other words, if you are going to give up the prospects of a future secured with social and financial success, then believe what you say, practice what you preach, and apply yourself in earnest. These words, emphasizing the importance of professional integrity, practical relevance, and personal industry became the guiding principles for my dad's ministry.

With this story as our context, what then can be said about genuine spiritual growth? I believe it says that real Christianity and genuine spiritual growth can be gauged by the cultivation of a closer relationship with God through the practice of spiritual disciplines and evidenced by open expressions of heartfelt Christian love. Beyond this, there is another determinant of authenticity that is often neglected or denied in contemporary theologies. That is the deference to God's will, whatever it may be. God always answers our prayers. Sometimes God's answer is yes, but sometimes God's answer is no. The willingness to defer to any divine expression, while continuing in one's Christian labor, is a fundamental determinant and clear evidence of authentic spiritual growth. A right relationship with God is preferable to a prayer answered according to our own personal desires.

The virtues of patience, long-suffering, endurance, forbearance, and humility are key indicators in taking a personal inventory that can also be applied to corporate ministry. If I am working in one direction and I see God working in a different direction, it is better for me to adjust my life to what God is doing rather than ask God to adjust what he is doing.[17] The victory of God in our lives is more in our continued faith in God than it is in God doing what we want God to do. This is not to discount the blessings that come from God. God's blessings, promises, prosperity, increase, and abundance are soundly biblical and factually real for all of those who trust and believe in God. I give praises of thanksgiving for the blessings of the Lord and look for them daily.

But what the spiritually authentic person who is growing in grace and godliness realizes is that blessings can come in unexpected ways that we never could have anticipated. "We know that all things work together for good for those who love God, who are called according to his purpose" (Rom. 8:28). When this understanding of divine operation is immersed in a spiritual perspective on life and contextualized by Christian principles and practice, it becomes a great strength to persevere in love and faith. As my dad used to say, "Whatever the Lord does is all right."

NINE

Seven Paths to Your Best Ministry Now!

Now there are varieties of gifts, but the same Spirit; and there are
varieties of services, but the same Lord. — 1 CORINTHIANS 12:4–5

THIS CHAPTER WILL LIST and expound on seven personal characteristics and behaviors that can enhance the ministry techniques
previously outlined. In the metaphor of building construction, the
previous techniques are the bricks, or the solid components, of local
church ministry. Applying them can result in an increase in attendance, tithes and offerings, and organizational success. The seven
personal traits that follow are the mortars that hold the techniques
together. They will afford the ministry a greater ability to endure
and sustain itself when it encounters the inevitable spiritual attacks
and hardships.

I have avoided using much scripture in the previous chapters. This
was deliberate so to avoid sermonizing the suggestions in this book.
These techniques are not absolutely perfect or universally applicable. They are suggestions and recommendations that generally can
be applied to at least some aspects of most parish ministries. In
order to be fully effective, they must be customized to the unique
setting, demographics, and personality of the congregation in which
they are introduced. In this chapter I will utilize more scriptures
to affirm these suggestions and establish them as beneficial ministerial methodologies. I believe that they are thoughts and actions
that always result in the pleasure and favor of God. It could be said
that these offerings are so obvious that they afford no addition to
the knowledge base of successful ministry and that they are simply
points of common sense. To this I would respond with the words
of Voltaire: "Common sense is not so common." The shortcoming of
most how-to books is that they really tell what to do, but not how to

do it. These points are critical in ensuring that the statistical increase promised in the previous chapters is actually realized, thus ensuring the personal relief of the ministry leader, the victory of the church ministry, and the glory of God!

One / Develop a Spiritual Perspective

The reason I speak to them in parables is that seeing they do not perceive, and hearing they do not listen, nor do they understand.

— MATTHEW 13:13

Developing a spiritual perspective on life and ministry is a prerequisite of spiritual maturity. Spiritual maturity is evidenced by being Christ-like. The more like Christ we are, the more spiritually mature we are. What, then, is a spiritual perspective? The spiritual perspective is best explained by expanding on the basic reason that you are reading this book. From a physical perspective, you are reading, and I am writing, this book so that you will have more people in church and have more resources whereby to perform ministry. That is the physical purpose for this book that can be quantifiably evaluated. But the spiritual perspective on this book would be that through it, God is working in our lives and the lives of all those around us, so that we may all become more like Christ. That would be the spiritual perspective and the spiritual victory of this book. Physical statistics may indicate the spiritual perspective and the spiritual perspective may affect the physical statistics, but they remain distinguished from each other.

When we engage the spiritual perspective in how we view ourselves and the community in which we minister, then we see God's hand in everything. We recognize God's divine presence and intervention all around us. Engaging the spiritual perspective means looking for and acknowledging God's divine omnipresence. "In all your ways acknowledge him, and he will make straight your paths" (Prov. 3:6). We see confrontations as spiritual warfare rages on spiritual planes rather than as conflicts with society or other persons. "For our struggle is not against enemies of blood and flesh, but against the rulers, against the authorities, against the cosmic powers of this present darkness, against the spiritual forces of evil in the heavenly places" (Eph. 6:12).

Engaging the spiritual perspective allows the recommendations of Christ to be more intense and urgent. "We must work the works of him who sent me while it is day; night is coming when no one can work" (John 9:4). When we cultivate a spiritual view of life, then our witness becomes more effective in pointing people to Christ. "But you will receive power when the Holy Spirit has come upon you; and you shall be my witnesses" (Acts 1:8). Church leaders with such a witness enhance the identification of the church as a divine representation in its community. As Henry Blackaby says in *Experiencing God*, "What the world is often seeing today is devoted, committed Christians serving God. But they are not seeing God."

A simple story may give more insight into the spiritual perspective. I call this the story of the Holy Roller. An old gray-haired lady, dressed in an ankle-length, loose dress with white sweat-socks and sandals, walks into her corner grocery to do her regular shopping. Everyone knows her and she greets everyone with a cheerful, "Bless you, dear!" She proceeds with her shopping cart into the store to the aisle that holds the items for which she is shopping. As she peruses the shelves and just as she is about to make her selection, her cell phone rings. Some small family emergency interrupts her shopping, and she hurries home. She returns the next day and repeats her familiar process. As she again peruses the items in the aisle in which she was interrupted the previous day, she suddenly erupts in a loud burst of praises of thanksgiving. Her chorus of hallelujahs is so excited and the commotion is so great, that over the intercom an anxious voice shouts, "Emergency in aisle nine!"

The employees rush to the aisle to surround her and settle her down. When they finally get her calmed down, they ask her if she is all right and what is going on. She constrains herself long enough to tell them, "Yesterday, I was here shopping for ketchup and the price was a dollar a bottle, but I couldn't get any because I had to rush home. Today I come back and the same bottle of ketchup is on sale for seventy-five cents! Hallelujah!" And with that she erupts all over again.

The Holy Roller has the spiritual perspective on life. Her family emergency of the previous day was the physical manifestation of divine intervention. The spiritual purpose was that God wanted to bless her faith by arranging for her to get a better price on ketchup. Her unrestricted praise was her faith response to God's blessing. She believes that everything that happens is a physical manifestation of a spiritual genesis. Her perspective on life is a comprehensive acknowledgment of God's omnipresence and omnipotence. This story clearly exemplifies the goal of developing a spiritual perspective. "Somehow we must spiritually orient ourselves and learn to see things from God's perspective."[1]

How do we develop and cultivate the spiritual perspective? We develop it through training ourselves to look for God's activity throughout the course of our normal day. This discipline is centered in our prayer life. Prayer is defined as communication with God. Communication is both talking and listening. The spiritual perspective begins with training ourselves to do less talking and more listening to God. We want to hear God's voice and see God's activity in every daily occurrence. When I wake up every morning, I ask myself, "I wonder how God will speak to me today." I include in my morning prayers, "God, help me to hear your voice as you speak to me today. Please assist me in having the mind and the will to respond as you would have me to. Please be merciful and kind to me, as you always have been, but also help me to accept your will, no matter what."

Then, as I proceed through the day, I do so with the knowledge that God is constantly speaking to me and the preoccupation to recognize when this is occurring. When I began this discipline, God often had to shout at me through the experiences of my life in order to get my attention. Now I have grown to be able to discern subtle indicators and divine whispers from God. Oprah Winfrey refers to these as "Godwinks." I rejoice in the many wonderful victories I have experienced in my life through following these divine whispers. God no longer has to shout to get my attention. When God shouts, it is because I have missed or ignored an opportunity to hear and obey God's voice. Developing and maintaining the spiritual perspective is very rewarding. It brings a peculiar spiritual peace that can come only from a constant awareness that God is in complete control.

Two / Practice Spiritual Discipline

Be gracious to me, O Lord, for to you do I cry all day long.
— PSALM 86:3

In order to maintain a spiritual perspective and to remain in good spiritual heath, spiritual disciplines are essential.[2] Spiritual disciplines begin with the daily devotions of prayer and Bible study. They continue with weekly worship, lending assistance to persons in need, fasting, and tithing.

As the spiritual perspective opens our eyes to the continuum of God's activity all around us, the spiritually disciplined life helps us to personally know God. "The goal of God's activity is that we know him."[3] The scriptures are full of references to this ultimate goal of God's activity. Ezekiel 34:30 ends an entire passage on God's restoration of Israel, saying, "Then they will know that I, the Lord their God, am with them, and that they, the house of Israel, are My people, declares the Lord." Jesus expresses his disappointment with Philip for not coming to the knowledge of who Jesus was after they had spent so much time together. John 14:9 says, "Have I been so long with you, and yet, you have not come to know me, Philip?"

When we have the practice of spiritual disciplines regularly in our lives, our journey becomes one of growing in the knowledge of who God is. This informs and refines us as his servants. Through the practice of spiritual disciplines we are divinely directed in what our service to God should be. This is what distinguishes our divine call to ministry from our conversion experience. As Henry Blackaby affirms in *Experiencing God*, "Knowing God does not come through our programs and methods of ministry. Knowing God is the result of cultivating a personal relationship with God because God is not a process or an activity. God is a person."

Practicing spiritual disciplines does not happen easily or as a natural result of our salvation. We must, in our spiritual perspective, understand that we are participants in a spiritual conflict.

SPIRITUAL PRACTICE MAKES SPIRITUAL PERFECTION

Daily Prayer

✝ Private (in your home or where the spirit leads)

✝ Public (at church, restaurants, family gatherings)

Bible Study

✝ Private (daily, in your home or where the spirit leads)

✝ Public (at Sunday Church School or other group settings; Wednesday Bible Study, 7:15 p.m.)

Periodic Fasting

✝ Private (as God leads you)

✝ Public (with the church body every Wednesday, in the way God leads you)

Regular Worship

✝ Public (EVERY SUNDAY)

✝ Private (in your home on a regular basis or for special occasions)

Mission

✝ Active participation in Christian outreach ministry (using the gifts God gave you, working where God places you)

Tithing

✝ 10 percent of the first fruits belong to GOD. Don't forget the stewardship of time and talent.

If my people, who are called by my name,
will humble themselves and pray
and seek my face and turn from their wicked ways,
then will I hear from heaven and will forgive their sin
and will heal their land.
2 Chronicles 7:14

Active forces of evil are seeking on every hand to hinder our relationship with God. The adversary knows that the more we know God, the more we will come to trust and obey God. Ettinger and Neinast state in *The Long and Winding Road*, "To trust in God requires a listening heart, and a listening heart requires time." The enemy of God will cause various interruptions and disturbances in our lives to keep us from our spiritual disciplines. We must be intentional about our spiritual disciplines if we are to grow in our spiritual maturity. Spiritual growth requires commitment and time.[4] In order to practice our spiritual disciplines we must carve a space out of our busy lives to be quietly present with God.

The most prevalent pattern of spiritual development seems to be a daily time set aside for prayer and meditation.[5] Our lives are filled with daily rituals. We usually brush our teeth, shower, and dress in the same order every day. A routine of daily devotional time becomes like any other personal routine or ritual. When it becomes a part of us, then its interruption is uncomfortable and our inclination is to return to it. Sometimes our immersion into the challenges of life and ministry cause us to become self-dependent and spiritually drained. We are so busy providing the "spiritual bread" for others that we are not aware of our own need for spiritual nourishment.

In addition to daily devotions, at times total separation from our venue of ministry, our church, or our mission field is recommended. Sometimes physical distance can provide needed emotional distance and open up new channels for God's revelation.[6] Jesus would often go into the wilderness so that he could have uninterrupted communion with God. Separation from the rigors of our obligations so that we may focus on our spiritual disciplines can afford divine communion in a way that praying unceasingly in the midst of a busy schedule cannot.

Maintaining a regular routine of spiritual discipline has benefits that are not immediately evident. Rick Warren encourages us to "never stop learning."[7] Regular devotions, particularly in the case of Bible study, offer the opportunity for continued Christian education. Spiritual growth experiences, such as conferences, workshops, free expression rap sessions and encounter groups, formal school enrollment, hands-on mission work, and more can enhance the spiritual growth of any believer. Providing opportunities for and encouraging participation in personal spiritual growth experiences can be the difference between harmony and conflict in the church.

When progressive initiatives in the church come to the critical moments of making hard decisions, a congregational culture of practicing spiritual disciplines can make the difference between faithful unity and oppositional division. "A culture of discipline will compensate for company growth problems more than bureaucracy, planning, etc."[8] When spiritual growth opportunities are readily available in the church and there is some public accountability to them, disagreeable spirits are more easily convicted and suppressed. This results in optimizing the church's energy and resources in its Realm building efforts. God takes pleasure in such a church family. "Behold, how good and how pleasant it is for brothers to dwell together in unity!" (Ps. 133:1).

Three / Prioritize Ministry Efforts

But all things must be done decently and in order.
— 1 CORINTHIANS 14:40

Setting priorities has several advantages. It ensures that what is most important is always attended to. This allows you to optimize the positive results of your efforts. Setting priorities also sets a framework for organizing your responsibilities. With a framework of organization set through prioritizing your responsibilities, you are able to see through the complexity of your many obligations and maintain a focus on what you are trying to accomplish. I constantly maintain a daily to-do list. It always has from five to twelve things that I wish to accomplish that day. I am usually able to complete about 60 percent of the list each day. The next day's list begins with those things that went unfinished from the previous list. In this fashion, I am able to maintain progress in my personal and ministerial responsibilities and optimize my energy output while maintaining as low a stress level as possible.

When we set priorities for our ministerial efforts we afford ourselves an opportunity to give prayerful consideration to what we are doing. In this, we make time for God to provide us with appropriate direction. "In all your ways acknowledge him, and he will make straight your paths" (Prov. 3:6). Determining what is most important allows us to be good stewards of our time and energy and to avoid being wasteful with the resources made available to us. We can accomplish the greatest good when through the prayerful process of prioritization God is able to reveal to us what is most important. As my father used to say, "Don't major in minors."

The result of establishing an organization of our efforts that result from setting priorities cannot be overstated. It is a primary responsibility of any authority figure to arrange things in an order. Creation resonates with God's order of the universal spiral and the physical laws that maintain it. Spiritual order is revealed in divine instruction with the order of the Ten Commandments as its foundation. Setting priorities, making to-do lists, and optimizing our energy and our resources for Realm building work evidences godly admonition and ministerial integrity. "Our steps are made firm by the Lord, when he delights in our way" (Ps. 37:23).

A discipline of setting priorities allows us to be in the present and focus our energies on the task that is at hand. When we have not set priorities, and thereby ordered how we will address our work, we will waste energy by working on things that are not immediately important. We can also miss opportunities by not addressing time-sensitive issues expeditiously. There is an energy spill-off because of the confusion caused by having so many things on our minds. We can dwell on things that at the moment we can do nothing about. The result is that we don't give our best effort to the work with which we are currently engaged.

This same rationale applies to our lifestyle. We live in a world that revels in the egotism of multitasking. A popular form of evaluating our intellect and ability is based on how many things we can do simultaneously. This tendency causes our life experiences to be shallow because we do not afford ourselves the time that is necessary to fully realize each passing moment. "Because we are focused on what we will do next, we miss out on what we are doing now."[9] In terms of ministry, we expend valuable mental energy by juggling in our minds several things that we have to do. We could prioritize these things, utilize time management, and give our best effort to the most immediate task. Then we can proceed through our day not only doing a better job with the things that confront us, but also having a greater degree of peace as we work, knowing that everything will be addressed in its proper order.

The key to prioritizing our work is documentation. "Write everything down."[10] God gives us creative inspiration to assist and to direct us in our working for him. The flow of creative inspiration can be blocked by trying to remember the inspiration after it has arrived. When we immediately record thoughts and ideas pertaining to the various items on our to-do list, then that will release our mental receptors to receive further inspiration and information. This practice keeps us from intellectually blocking our own blessings. "For where two or three are gathered in my name, I am there among them" (Matt. 18:20).

Organizing ministry efforts often necessitates team building. Team building, though challenging for some persons, is an effective method in performing ministry. Though pastors, ministers, or church leaders may sometimes find themselves feeling alone, Christian ministry is not and never has been a Lone Ranger operation. From Noah to Moses to Jesus to Paul, building a team has always been crucial in effective ministry. No one can do everything that the Lord requires of him by working alone. Sometimes the Lord will send us into lonely wilderness places. God uses isolation and solitude as a way of building our faith. But God does not require that we be left alone in doing his work. In order to realize the broad visions of ministry and to specifically address daily responsibilities, the minister must build a team.[11]

Team building can accomplish much. It helps a ministry with priorities fulfill its responsibilities, thereby becoming more effective. It also affords persons other than the ministry leader the opportunity to make contributions to Realm building and to grow in their faith. The ministry leader greatly benefits in a spiritual sense through this indirect blessing because as other persons successfully carry out tasks, the leader then must often share the limelight. This helps to keep the leader humble, and the authentic spiritual integrity of the minister can be preserved. After all, it's not about us, it's about Jesus. An ambition for Realm building and not for self aggrandizement is constantly reinforced by working with a team. President Harry S. Truman once said, "You can accomplish anything in life, as long as you don't care who gets the credit."[12] Jim Collins says in *Good to Great,* "Great people have a moral code for excellence, not reward."

When we consider team building in a church setting, the team likely will consist of both volunteers and paid staff. In most cases, the team will begin with volunteers and then progress into paid staff positions. I use a simple rule when establishing a paid staff position. When a job that is being done by a volunteer becomes so crucial to the ministry that the absence of the volunteer will noticeably diminish the ministry, then it is time to consider making that job a paid position. Most volunteers give service because they enjoy what they are doing. Their service gives them a sense of fulfillment. If, however, they have no compensation accountability for performing their duties, then sometimes they will not be available. Their job, family, or other personal priorities will intervene.

Paying a staff establishes a salary scale for the church. The church salaries should be commensurate with the jobs being performed, the geographic location of the church, and the ability of the church to pay the salaries.[13] For corporate comparisons of salary scales, churches are not-for-profit agencies. This means that the salaries in a church will be somewhat lower in most cases than in the corporate sector. There are, however, are a lot of fringe benefits in working for a church that are not available in the corporate sector. These benefits can make up for a slightly lower pay scale. Such things as the Christian atmosphere of the church, a greater flexibility of work schedules, increased access to various spiritual growth activities, and a unique sense of personal fulfillment can bring a joy and a peace to a church employee that a corporate job cannot.

Whether a person is a volunteer or a paid staff member, he or she is a part of the ministry team. The ministry team is on the front line of servant leadership. They are the persons ensuring that effective ministry occurs for the congregation and for the community. The importance of an effective team cannot be overemphasized if your church is to have dynamic ministry. "If your church is to sustain growth momentum, staffing must become a very high priority."[14]

Now that an effective team is in place and ministry is going forth in an orderly fashion, the church leader can be assured that the resources of the church are being optimized. They are not being unnecessarily diverted from ministry in order to support an ineffective administration. It is important that the church as an incorporated entity with fiscal and service responsibilities operates with good business principles. The busy-ness of the church should not primarily be invested in the administrative business of the church. It should be invested in effecting Christian ministry. The essence of Christian ministry is not the building of church facilities, the development of programs, or being involved in activities. It is not even the encouragement of people's spirits or relieving their personal distress. The core value and the primary purpose of Christian ministry is to help persons become more like Jesus.

It is easy to be distracted from the primary goal of Christ with the subordinate business activities of the church. These activities are certainly ministries in themselves and necessary to the overall victory of Christ and his church, but they are still systems and processes that support the goal of ministry. They are not the goal of ministry itself. A prime example is the process of how I have authored this book. I have written this book under the constant urging of the Holy Spirit, and I believe in my heart that it will be a blessing to some Christian soldier. This book, however, has taken me five years to complete. To some degree it is because of vacillating levels of personal commitment throughout the writing process. But to a larger degree it is because I have given a higher priority to my responsibilities as a pastor. There was always a telephone call, a hospital visit, a counseling session, or a meeting that would cause a break in the continuous progress of my writing. Even though I felt an undeniable urging of the Spirit to complete this book, my pastoral duties always took precedence.

I don't mention this to bolster the victory of this book's completion or to elevate my pastoral calling over the importance of writing the book. The point I am making is that my pastoral duties and the writing of this book existed within a set of priorities that assisted me in the organization and fulfillment of my work. Even Jesus operated with a set of priorities. "Jesus did not spend his time creating operations manuals that could be franchised and duplicated by the millions. He hurried to see a little girl who was sick."[15] Jesus readily communicated his priorities when decisions were made regarding his ministry. "But he had to go through Samaria" (John 4:4).

I commend all of the authoring pastors who are prolific writers. The spiritual admonition to write is an added burden to the already daunting task of being a pastor. All pastors and church leaders will operate more effectively with a set of priorities that continuously evolves as current tasks are completed and new tasks are added.

Finally, an important point remains regarding priorities for the pastor or ministry leader. Take time for personal care and for the care of your family. So often pastors and their families suffer because of the demands of pastoral responsibilities. Because of the professional, emotional, and spiritual investment related to pastoring, "Pastors and their spouses and children face some unique problems."[16] The pastor's family is scrutinized like that of no other public or professional leader. Pastors, therefore, for their own health and for the health of their family, must "spend more time for rest, exercise, recreation, to be with family or friends, or to engage in outside activities."[17] Jesus was a good steward of his family and of his personal energy. His disciples often found him praying alone to his heavenly Father in the early hours. He continued in an interactive and responsible relationship with his human family throughout his entire ministry. "For if someone does not know how to manage his own household, how can he take care of God's church?" (1 Tim. 3:5). Taking personal care of yourself and of your family is a scriptural mandate in performing ministry.

Four / Maintain a Self-Care Discipline

The angel of the Lord came a second time, touched him, and said, "Get up and eat, otherwise the journey will be too much for you."

— 1 KINGS 19:7

This book's primary purpose is to assist in facilitating a statistically quantifiable improvement in your ministry. Its goal is to increase the number of persons you have in worship, the tithes and offerings you receive, and your joy in performing ministry. My hope is that the suggestions offered here will help your congregation to be the dynamic and effective ministry that God desires. In order to accomplish this, there are three resources that your congregation must have: disciplined people, disciplined thought, and disciplined action.[18]

One of the benefits of a culture of discipline is that it encourages good stewardship of ministry resources and personal energy. This is absolutely necessary for pastors and church leaders. "Jesus guarded his energy."[19] I used to hear my professors talking about burnout while I was in seminary. I was so full of vim and vigor that I wondered what it was. Some twenty years later, however, as a pastor, I finally experienced burnout. Six months after we completed the construction of DuPage's new worship facility, I was truly burned out. I was tired all the time regardless of how much I slept. I was grouchy with everyone. When you are burned out, you are of little help to anybody. Our family went on an extended vacation, and I returned refreshed and renewed.

Donald Smith defines burnout as well as anyone in *Empowering Ministry*, stating, "Burnout is the loss of energy, purpose, and idealism that results from excessive unmanaged stress in our work." When pastors or ministry leaders reach burnout, they are more counterproductive than productive as regards the ministry. A lifestyle of discipline as regards our spiritual devotions, ministry efforts, and family obligations must include a necessary component of self-care. Pastors and ministry leaders must understand that "leadership skills include caring for oneself."[20] If you are going to last in ministry, you must understand and accept that, as C. Jeff Woods reminds in *Better Than Success: 8 Principles of Faithful Leadership*, "All long-term leaders take care of themselves."

Lifestyle discipline is not particular solely to time management, resource stewardship, and self-care. Lifestyle discipline, for the pastor or ministry leader, is a vehicle to exemplify Christian character. As soldiers on the spiritual battlefield, we must always be aware that we are subject to attacks from the devil, our spiritual adversary. These attacks are intended to "steal and kill and destroy" our ministry (John 10:10). Setting priorities and practicing disciplines serve to undergird us as we continue in Christian service. In 1 Corinthians 9:27, Paul says, "But I punish my body and enslave it, so that after proclaiming to others I myself should not be disqualified."

As we work with God to save the world, we also work with God to save ourselves.[21] When our ministries are progressing victoriously and God's blessings are abundantly flowing, we must be even more vigilant in our disciplines. Sometimes ministry effectiveness can lull us into thinking that what we do for God is more important than who we are in God. This is a false presumption. We can have great discipline as regards the ministry and yet become less vigilant about our own spiritual and physical well-being. God's plan for salvation is holistic. First, it addresses persons as individuals. It expands to include our households and the community in which we live. But the expansion of God's salvation to us as individuals extends to the full nature of who we are as human beings. "I would that you be in good health, even as your soul prospers" (3 John 2). In our divine calling to Christian ministry we are also called to a lifestyle of discipline that preserves us in our service. I offer the physical fitness imperatives of daily exercise and a healthy diet, along with getting the proper rest, relaxation, and recreation.

Five / Express Engaging Kindness

I give you a new commandment, that you love one another. Just as I have loved you, you also should love one another.   — JOHN 13:34

Love is the greatest weapon we have in the battle to win souls for Christ. Love is the essence of Christian character. Its expression is the most powerful technique in furthering Christian ministry. "Genuine caring is the engine in each local church that propels its growth."[22]

Pastors and members often talk about relationships in their church. It is not uncommon when the discussion settles on a particular person or group to hear, "I passed them and they didn't even speak to me." My response is always the same. "Did you speak to them? Did you go up and smile, and hug them? Did you offer your hand in fellowship?" I know that persons can be rude, and even downright mean at times.

This is why the agape love of a Christian is so special. Love and courteous expressions are nice to receive, but the Christian is not called to receive them. The Christian is called to share them. "Love one another, as I have loved you!" (John 15:12). In his book *Twelve Dynamic Shifts for Transforming Your Church*, E. Stanley Ott says, "If we want new persons to join our churches, hospitality must be practiced on a personal basis." More specifically, if pastors or ministry leaders want to increase the effectiveness of their ministry, they must initiate hospitable greetings and courtesies at every possible opportunity. Don't wait for people to speak to you. In fact, don't even give them the chance. Always beat them to it with your own personal greeting. When you enter your church, no matter how preoccupied you are or how important the meeting you are rushing to is, if there are people there, take time to graciously greet everyone. For me, this is a cornerstone of the pastorate and a spiritual gift that I enjoy exercising. It has paid greater dividends in God's blessing of our ministry than all of the dreams, visions, campaigns, and programs combined.

Engaging kindness is an indispensable component of authentic Christian ministry. It is also a starting point for effective Christian leadership. Many pastors and ministry leaders have great dreams, goals, and visions for their churches. One of the challenges of manifesting vision is in getting the congregation to take ownership of the vision and support the leadership. Many visionary ideas have either failed, languished unfulfilled for many years, or resulted in outright congregational rebellion and the removal of the pastor because the pastor attempted to move the congregation to action before establishing a caring pastoral relationship. Christian people respond much better to a leader who they know is concerned about them. Because Jesus loved people and met their individual and personal needs, he was then able to teach and lead them in interesting and practical ways.[23] Many wise pastors have said, and as Smith clearly articulates in *Empowering Ministry*, "Show them you love them before you lead them." "People don't care how much you know until they know how much you care."[24] The success of pastoral ministry is not so much based on the intelligence quotient of the pastor, nor any other personal aspect, so much as it is on the pastor's capacity to be compassionate. The pastor or ministry leader must openly show genuine affection to those whom God has sent him to serve.

This outward display of enthusiastic fellowship may have to be exercised for many weeks, months, and even years before the congregation comes to accept it as genuine. Showing love cannot be a means to an end, or a way to get things done. That would be unethical. Showing love must be an end in itself. When it results in a more effective ministry, a ministry with a visible and tangible increase, this divine confirmation is an indirect blessing. I emphasize the personal attribute of engaging kindness because it is so important for the success of ministry, but it cannot be faked or pretentious. As time passes and the ongoing life of the congregation progresses, the heart of the pastor surely will be proven.

Many pastors have grown cynical because of repeatedly hearing unkind words from a congregation, and many congregations have been emotionally injured because of the uncaring actions of a pastor. These all had their beginning in someone's inauthentic affection and feigned Christian love. Pastors must understand that it is hard to get into the caring level of most churches.[25] In most cases, it takes patience and long-suffering. My strongest suggestion for any pastor is to love the congregation openly. Consider their life struggle and be as kind to them as possible. Give them leadership but make loving them the ministerial priority. God will bless the ministry. Keep showing love, be patient, and wait on the Lord to move the hearts of the congregation. Pray that God's vision becomes manifest, and then watch God move your ministry to greater spiritual and tangible yields.

Six / Cultivate Patience with Understanding

> *. . . you must make every effort to support your faith with goodness, and goodness with knowledge, and knowledge with self-control, and self-control with endurance, and endurance with godliness, and godliness with mutual affection, and mutual affection with love.*
>
> — 2 PETER 1:5–7

I have just expressed to you the need for engaging members with kindness by initiating courteous greetings at every opportunity. I encourage you to practice this until it is appropriated into your leadership style. The importance of this cannot be overemphasized. Even though as pastors and ministry leaders we have some measure of the gift of discernment, we don't know everything about the people to whom we minister. We do not know each member's physical, emotional, and spiritual condition. We do not know his or her total life experience or how it impacts the season of life that he or she is presently in.

Each person's perspective is based on his or her own life experience and sometimes leaders project their own personal perspectives onto those who follow them. It is an error for church leaders to assume that the members of their congregation see the world as they do. It is an error to assume that the congregation understands and interprets words in the way that they do. To make such presumptions is a recipe for failure. This proposition underscores my pastoral theology that spirituality must meet practicality. In Christ, God became flesh and lived among us (John 1:14). In doing this, he met human beings where we were. This is not evidence of a divine compromise in salvation history. It is rather an acknowledgment that divinity and humanity are different.

Therefore, the difference must be bridged in order to create a communal connection and to provide the opportunity for salvation. The same is true in pastoring. The only difference is that God knows our condition completely, while we are not completely knowledgeable of who our members are, how they came to be that way, or how they interpret the information we give them. Smith affirms this viewpoint in *Empowering Ministry*, saying, "Be kind because you never know what the other person is going through."

The first challenge I faced at DuPage was to reconcile a dispute within the music department. There were loyal members on both sides of the issue. I met with several persons and groups in the process of seeking a resolution. One meeting in particular did not end on a positive note. For many years when I recalled that meeting my spirit would resonate with a sense of failure. I was meeting with a member who was passionately expressing her point of view. In response, I gave her what I thought was a very clear and rational way of looking at how we were addressing the situation.

To my surprise, she took my comments as a personal affront. We both felt strained, awkward, and uncomfortable as we ended that meeting. Often persons in crisis about their church involvement will come to the pastor to be heard, not to be helped. In such cases, being heard is being helped. It would have been much better if I had simply received her with prayerful consideration rather than attempting to convince her of a solution. Blanchard and the Robinsons' statement in *Zap the Gaps* can be appropriated from its retail setting and applied to a church setting: "Exhibit patience and allow the customer to vent." Sometimes it's best just to let the member vent. The best solution is not always what can be done about a situation but rather simply allowing the pressure of the situation to be released.

There is a practical benefit to exercising patient constraint. An old adage says, "There are two sides to every story." I continue to be amazed at how different persons can have different viewpoints on the same subject. The different involvements, investments, and priorities people have concerning an issue will determine their varying opinions regarding it. Patience allows the pastor or ministry leader to do what any person in a position of authority should do before making decisions, and that is to get all of the facts before acting.[26]

God is always ready to bless us. When we are tested by some tribulation, it's possible that we have fallen under some demonic spiritual attack. The enemy is constantly active, seeking ways to keep us from being blessed. Affliction, however, is not always the result of spiritual attack. Sometimes God allows our faith to be tested in order to confirm our readiness to receive a blessing in the way that God desires. A common test of faith that God allows is the test of being able to show agape love. God often sends pastors and ministers to people who are difficult to love.

God wants to use ministers to break down that person's difficulties so that the love of Christ may be shared with him or her. This is one of the methods God uses in leading persons to salvation. The sad truth is that most people have never experienced unconditional love and acceptance. They have only known conditional love.[27] When love suffers long and is kind, it allows wounded, hurting Christians and unsaved persons who are candidates for salvation to experience the truth of God's love and desire for their redemption.

In our culture of immediate gratification, we want to see the miracles of victorious ministry occur overnight. We want the fruits of our efforts to spring forth from our congregations even as the seeds of faith are being planted. In most success stories, however, it is persistence and perseverance that eventually result in success. The victory of some ministries may appear to be immediate, but it is usually the result of extended labor and arduous sacrifice that was unseen prior to their visible success. As Jim Collins says in *Good to Great,* "The good to great transformation happens not in a fell swoop, but from a process of relentless pushing."

When we look at ministry from the reference point of the spiritual perspective, the personality of the pastor or ministry leader as regards what is necessary to effect these implementations begins to coalesce. There are a number of personality types and a number of tests to determine them, like Myers-Briggs and others. The question is, what type of person can successfully employ these suggestions so that they result in the measurable increase of the local church ministry? The charismatic leader and the dynamic evangelist are the prevailing personas who have historically been able to bring about these results. In today's evolving culture, these personas continue to provide models of leadership for church growth and ministry development.

Certain problems, however, surface with the exclusive application of these leadership models in the church setting. One problem is that every pastor or ministry leader does not have the spiritual gifts of charisma or evangelistic preaching. Another problem is that church growth and Realm growth are two different things. Experienced pastors are aware that having a large number of persons on the church roll does not necessarily equate with a spiritually mature church. If being on the roll were sufficient, God would not have required the lamb's sacrificial blood on the doorposts of the Hebrews as a sign for the Passover. God knew what neighborhood the Israelites lived in. God knew their addresses. God could simply have instructed the death angel to pass over every Hebrew as a matter of course.

The lamb's blood was a sign of obedience. It was required because being a Hebrew did not guarantee obedience to God. The Apostle Paul affirms this in Romans 2:29, "Rather, a person is a Jew who is one inwardly, and real circumcision is a matter of the heart — it is spiritual and not literal."

Rather than depend on leadership models that are specific to particular gifts, the suggestions in this book are offered with the belief that they can be applied successfully by any minister. The only characteristic necessary for the effective application of these suggestions is that of humility. The pastor or ministry leader must accept the premise that progressive and positive ministry results are more important than being in charge and knowing more than everybody else. As a pastor or ministry leader, you are already in charge. Being God's representative, you certainly have knowledge that others do not have. But God does not send pastors and ministry leaders to be in charge and to know more than everybody else. God sends them to minister to the needs of the people and to facilitate the growth of God's Realm.

A story is told of a young new pastor who wanted to establish himself as the leader of a congregation. Every time he preached, chaired a meeting, taught a Bible study, or held a conversation, he remarked to whoever was listening, "I am the pastor." The internal life of the church soon became one of confrontation and division. Every auxiliary of the church was affected. It seemed that an argument ensued when any issue was discussed in the church. One Sunday after service, in speaking to one of the senior ladies of the church, the young man once again pressed a point by reminding her that he was the pastor. She candidly looked the young man in the eye and responded, "That's why everything around here is in a mess, because you *is* the pastor."

In the average setting of the majority of Christian congregations today, the old-school form of dictatorial leadership is no longer effective. Most people today do not respond to this type of leadership. There is a broad and diverse array of churches in which persons may join and participate. There are too many avenues to heaven for persons to submit themselves to oppressive leadership. There is no longer that kind of loyalty to specific denominations or local churches. Progressive leaders today are in most cases more humble than willful. They will find creative ways to motivate the congregation, ways that are not based solely in the authority of their leadership position. Jim Collins expresses this same sentiment about the corporate sector, saying, "Good to great leaders are self-effacing, quiet, reserved, shy, a paradoxical blend of humanity and professional will."[28] Jesus taught this same leadership style: "The Son of Man came not to be served but to serve" (Matt. 20:28a).

Seven / Acceptance

Let it be with me according to your word.
— LUKE 1:38

Being an effective Christian leader requires faith, and I believe that exercising faith requires a willingness to accept God's will in every circumstance. I do not mean this in the sense of acquiescing to defeat. What I mean is that whenever we desire a change in a situation, we must join the acceptance of the situation with the prayer of faith where God is invited to intervene and to transform the reality of that situation. Denial is a barrier to faith. Denial of the undesirable reality dismisses the reality and consequently removes the need for God to change that reality. An acceptance of such a reality leads to petitions for God to intervene. Acceptance can be viewed as the access point of faith.[29]

Many times we deny situations that need changing because we feel that by acknowledging them we are somehow being unfaithful. We immediately begin claiming the victory of the desired and envisioned reality. We immediately begin "to call into existence the things that do not exist" (Rom. 4:17). In doing this before we fully acknowledge the undesirable reality, we miss a crucial step in our faith walk, and that is the step of acceptance. Acceptance is the step in which we see where a miracle is needed, then "become still and know that he is God" (Ps. 46:10).

Missing this step causes us to skip over the pivotal time of spiritual mobilization. This is our prayer time, when we muster all of our faith, obedience, and patience. We begin envisioning the victory of an undesirable reality being transformed and then claiming that envisioned transformation as we walk in faith. Undesirable situations arise as results of demonic spiritual attack. They also arise from God's initiation to test our faith or to strengthen our faith. Someone once asked me, "What is the difference between spiritual attack and a test from God?" God revealed to me that, although both of those circumstances may look the same, the purpose of each is different. Spiritual attacks occur for the purpose of destroying us. Divine tests occur for the purpose of bringing us to salvation and strengthening our faith. It may be God's will that we are in a situation. God may be preparing us for some challenge yet to come. Henry Blackaby says in *Experiencing God,* "If you really believe that God is love, then you will also accept that his will is best."

Another reason we shy away from the acceptance of undesirable situations is because they are humbling experiences. Being in a situation of brokenness acknowledges that we are not perfect nor are we completely in control. It shows that our ability and our faith have not afforded us absolution from trouble. Sometimes we rationalize the situation in order to make it fit our self-perceptions. Sometimes we project the blame for the situation onto someone or something else. We forget the divine principle that "God exalts whoever humbles themselves."[30]

Accepting reality, particularly when it is undesirable, is the first step toward the victory of prayerfully changing that reality through faith in God. Jesus always asked a petitioner, "What do you want me to do?" He did this even when the affliction was obvious. Acknowledging the conditions was the first step in their faith to believe that Jesus could change their conditions. When God answers the prayer of faith with victory and the undesirable circumstances are overcome, then we experience the unspeakable joy of a true miracle. An old gospel song says, "The storm is passing over." A praise hymn echoes, "I'm so glad, that trouble don't last always." Authentic Christian theology does not deny the storm or ignore the trouble. It proves faith by believing that God is truly able to bring peace and resolution. The praises of thanksgiving that follow the miraculous change are then unstoppable. "He answered, 'I tell you, if these were silent, the stones would shout out'" (Luke 19:40).

This leads us back to the primary aspect of servanthood, which is to assist in bringing about what God desires. We are Realm servants and therefore must see not only the small picture of our immediate condition, but also the larger picture of world redemption and eschatological conclusion. Jeff Woods articulates this point most clearly in *Better than Success: 8 Principles of Faithful Leadership*, saying, "Successful leaders have a need to be in front. Faithful leaders have a need to follow God." God directs the victory and the people are called to follow God's direction through the servant leadership of their pastor or ministry leader. "Individual opinions are not that important. The will of God is very important."[31]

Acceptance of reality, especially when that reality may be the last thing that the servant of God wants, is the ultimate act of humility and obedience. It is the will of God concerning you. But I again emphasize that acceptance is not an acquiescence to defeat. It is a bold faith expression that God is able to bring victory. Shadrach, Meshach, and Abednego made such a bold faith expression to King Nebuchadnezzar, saying, "If our God whom we serve is able to deliver us from the furnace of blazing fire and out of your hand, O king, let him deliver us. But if not, be it known to you, O king, that we will not serve your gods and we will not worship the golden statue that you have set up" (Dan. 3:17–18).

At DuPage, we sing a praise hymn that affirms such faith entitled "Hallelujah Anyhow!" Faith stands in the face of total impossibility and becomes the catalyst for divine intervention. Miraculous change follows in the fullness of time. Then our testimonies are bolder and our praises more fervent. Our faith grows and becomes more steadfast because we have a sure understanding of what the Lord can and will do.

Conclusion

I have a testimony to give. I love being a pastor and, I am so glad that I do. When we love what we are doing it enhances our ability to reach our full potential. In terms of a person's life work, my father always said, "It's not how much money you make, but it's what you do with what you make and how you enjoy what you do."

It is my prayer that some of the contents of this book can be appropriated into your local church ministry, resulting in visible, tangible, and substantial increases in resources and effectiveness. More than anything else, I pray that every pastor, minister, and church member will grow in the love of their Christian callings, so that they may enjoy the ministry with which God has entrusted them. There can be no denying that Christian ministry is much labor. Christian ministry is arduous and exacting work. May the God who neither slumbers nor sleeps strengthen you in every good work, and may your communion with God be your victory and your testimony.

Notes

Preface

1. C. Jeff Woods, *Better Than Success: 8 Principles of Faithful Leadership* (Valley Forge, Pa.: Judson Press, 1989), 85.

Chapter 1: Evangelism

1. Rick Warren, *The Purpose-Driven Church* (Grand Rapids: Zondervan, 1995), 139.
2. Carl F. George, *Prepare Your Church for the Future* (Grand Rapids: Fleming H. Revell, 1992), 172.
3. Warren, *The Purpose-Driven Church*, 173.
4. George, *Prepare Your Church for the Future*, 85.
5. Kennon L. Callahan, *Twelve Keys to an Effective Church* (San Francisco: Harper, 1983), 24–25.
6. Charles Arn, *How to Start a New Service* (Grand Rapids: Baker, 1997), 217.
7. Alan Nelson and Stan Toler, *The Five-Star Church* (Ventura, Calif.: Regal Books, 1999), 137.
8. Ibid., 76.
9. Warren, *The Purpose-Driven Church*, 166.
10. Ibid., 65.
11. Ibid., 40.
12. Ibid., 311.
13. Henry Blackaby and Claude V. King, *Experiencing God* (Nashville: Lifeway Press, 1990), 141.

Chapter 2: Administration

1. Rick Warren, *The Purpose Driven Church* (Grand Rapids: Zondervan, 1995), 96.
2. Kennon L. Callahan, *Twelve Keys to an Effective Church* (San Francisco: Harper, 1983), 78.
3. C. Jeff Woods, *Better Than Success: 8 Principles of Faithful Leadership* (Valley Forge, Pa.: Judson Press, 1989), 91.
4. Henry Blackaby and Claude V. King, *Experiencing God* (Nashville: Lifeway Press, 1990), 55.
5. Warren, *The Purpose-Driven Church*, 345.
6. George Barna, *Marketing the Church* (Colorado Springs: Navpress, 1988), 88.
7. Callahan, *Twelve Keys to an Effective Church*, 59.

8. Woods, *Better than Success*, 88.

9. Rick Warren, *Spiritual Authority* (New York: Christian Fellowship Publishers, 1972), 120.

Chapter 3: Stewardship

1. George Barna, *The Habits of Highly Effective Churches* (Ventura, Calif.: Regal Books, 1999), 144.

2. C. Jeff Woods, *Better Than Success: 8 Principles of Faithful Leadership* (Valley Forge, Pa.: Judson Press, 1989), 82.

Chapter 4: Raising the Church Budget

1. George Barna, *The Habits of Highly Effective Churches* (Ventura, Calif.: Regal Books, 1999), 14.

2. Gary L. McIntosh, *Staff Your Church for Growth* (Grand Rapids: Baker, 2000), 13.

3. George Barna, *Marketing the Church* (Colorado Springs, Colo.: Navpress, 1988), 23.

4. C. Jeff Woods, *Better Than Success: 8 Principles of Faithful Leadership* (Valley Forge, Pa.: Judson Press, 1989), 15.

5. Alan Nelson and Stan Toler, *The Five-Star Church* (Ventura, Calif.: Regal Books, 1999), 201.

6. McIntosh, *Staff Your Church*, 81.

7. Floyd R. Massey Jr. and Samuel Berry McKinney, *Church Administration in the Black Perspective* (Valley Forge, Pa.: Judson Press, 1976), 58.

8. Nelson and Toler, *The Five-Star Church*, 45.

9. McIntosh, *Staff Your Church*, 121.

10. Carl F. George, *Prepare Your Church for the Future* (Grand Rapids: Fleming H. Revell, 1992), 33.

11. Watchman Nee, *Spiritual Authority* (New York: Christian Fellowship Publishers, 1972), 110.

12. Ken Blanchard, Dana Robinson, and Jim Robinson, *Zap the Gaps* (New York: William Morrow, 2002), xiv.

13. Rick Warren, *The Purpose-Driven Church* (Grand Rapids: Zondervan, 1995), 89.

14. George Barna, *The Frog in the Kettle* (Ventura: Regal Books, 1990), 44.

Chapter 5: Planning Capital Projects

1. C. Jeff Woods, *Better Than Success: 8 Principles of Faithful Leadership* (Valley Forge, Pa.: Judson Press, 1989), 92.

2. George Barna, *Marketing the Church* (Colorado Springs: Navpress, 1988), 118.

3. Charles Arn, *How to Start a New Service* (Grand Rapids: Baker, 1997), 43.

4. Henry Blackaby and Claude V. King, *Experiencing God* (Nashville: Lifeway Press, 1990), 178.

5. Ibid., 119.

6. "The Doctrine and Discipline of the African Methodist Episcopal Church," 2004 (Nashville: AMEC Sunday School Union, 2005), 70.

7. Woods, *Better than Success*, 126.

8. Barna, *Marketing the Church*, 52.

9. Floyd R. Massey Jr. and Samuel Berry McKinney, *Church Administration in the Black Perspective* (Valley Forge, Pa.: Judson Press, 1976), 111.

10. Barna, *Marketing the Church*, 90.

Chapter 6: Financing Capital Projects

1. Kennon L. Callahan, *Twelve Keys to an Effective Church* (San Francisco: Harper, 1983), xv.

2. Rick Warren, *The Purpose-Driven Church* (Grand Rapids: Zondervan, 1995), 94.

3. Henry Blackaby and Claude V. King, *Experiencing God* (Nashville: Lifeway Press, 1990), 7.

4. C. Jeff Woods, *Better Than Success: 8 Principles of Faithful Leadership* (Valley Forge, Pa.: Judson Press, 1989), 2.

Chapter 7: Worship

1. E. Stanley Ott, *Twelve Dynamic Shifts for Transforming Your Church* (Grand Rapids: William Eerdmans, 2002), 6.

2. George Barna, *The Habits of Highly Effective Churches* (Ventura, Calif.: Regal Books, 1999), 87.

3. George Barna, *The Frog in the Kettle* (Ventura, Calif.: Regal Books, 1990), 15.

4. Charles Arn, *How to Start a New Service* (Grand Rapids: Baker, 1997), 37.

5. Ott, *Twelve Dynamic Shifts for Transforming Your Church*, 90.

6. Ibid., 89.

7. Arn, *How to Start a New Service*, 19.

8. Rick Warren, *The Purpose-Driven Church* (Grand Rapids: Zondervan, 1995), 254.

9. Ibid., 255.

10. Ibid., 275.

11. Barna, *The Habits of Highly Effective Churches*, 38.

12. C. Jeff Woods, *Better Than Success: 8 Principles of Faithful Leadership* (Valley Forge, Pa.: Judson Press, 1989), 91.

13. Barna, *The Habits of Highly Effective Churches*, 113.

14. Ibid., 24.

15. Gary L. McIntosh, *Staff Your Church for the Future* (Grand Rapids: Baker, 2000), 70.

16. Warren, *The Purpose-Driven Church*, 51.

17. Barna, *The Habits of Highly Effective Churches*, 96.

18. Alan Nelson and Stan Toler, *The Five-Star Church* (Ventura, Calif.: Regal Books, 1999), 70.

19. Kennon L. Callahan, *Twelve Keys to an Effective Church* (San Francisco: Harper, 1983), 10.

20. Barna, *The Frog in the Kettle,* 94.
21. Henry Blackaby and Claude V. King, *Experiencing God* (Nashville: Lifeway Press, 1990), 55.
22. Barna, *The Frog in the Kettle,* 45.
23. Nelson and Toler, *The Five-Star Church,* 19.
24. Barna, *The Habits of Highly Effective Churches,* 83.

Chapter 8: Personal and Congregational Spiritual Growth

1. Henry Blackaby and Claude V. King, *Experiencing God* (Nashville: Lifeway Press, 1990), 8.
2. Alan Richardson, *A Dictionary of Christian Theology* (The Westminster Press, Philadelphia: 1969), 303.
3. Rick Warren, *The Purpose-Driven Church* (Grand Rapids: Zondervan, 1995), 331.
4. Blackaby and King, *Experiencing God,* 122.
5. C. Jeff Woods, *Better Than Success: 8 Principles of Faithful Leadership* (Valley Forge, Pa.: Judson Press, 1989), 72.
6. Ibid., v.
7. Donald P. Smith, *Empowering Ministry: Ways to Grow in Effectiveness* (Louisville: Westminster John Knox Press, 1996), 94.
8. Thomas C. Ettinger and Helen R. Neinast, *The Long and Winding Road* (Nashville: Dimensions, 1998), 12.
9. Ibid., 75.
10. Ibid., 14.
11. George Barna, *Marketing the Church* (Colorado Springs: Navpress, 1988), 17.
12. George Barna, *The Habits of Highly Effective Churches* (Ventura, Calif.: Regal Books, 1999), 12.
13. George Barna, *The Frog in the Kettle* (Ventura: Regal Books, 1990), 25.
14. Spencer Johnson, M.D., *Who Moved My Cheese?* (New York: G. P. Putnam Sons, 1998), 115
15. Alan Nelson and Stan Toler, *The Five-Star Church* (Ventura, Calif.: Regal Books, 1999), 10.
16. Barna, *The Habits of Highly Effective Churches,* 17.
17. Blackaby and King, *Experiencing God,* 92.

Chapter 9: Seven Paths to Your Best Ministry Now!

1. Henry Blackaby and Claude V. King, *Experiencing God* (Nashville: Lifeway Press, 1990), 32.
2. Donald P. Smith, *Empowering Ministry: Ways to Grow in Effectiveness* (Louisville: Westminster John Knox Press, 1996), 94.
3. Blackaby and King, *Experiencing God,* 39.
4. Rick Warren, *The Purpose-Driven Church* (Grand Rapids: Zondervan, 1995), 332.
5. Smith, *Empowering Ministry,* 94.
6. C. Jeff Woods, *Better Than Success: 8 Principles of Faithful Leadership* (Valley Forge, Pa.: Judson Press, 1989), 12.

7. Warren, *The Purpose-Driven Church*, 18.

8. Jim Collins, *Good to Great* (New York: Harper Business Press, 2001), 121.

9. Thomas C. Ettinger and Helen R. Neinast, *The Long and Winding Road* (Nashville: Dimensions, 1998), 12.

10. Warren, *The Purpose-Driven Church*, 98.

11. George Barna, *Marketing the Church* (Colorado Springs: Navpress, 1988), 126.

12. Collins, *Good to Great*, 21.

13. *The Doctrine and Discipline of the A.M.E. Church*, 68.

14. Gary L. McIntosh, *Staff Your Church for the Future* (Grand Rapids: Baker, 2000), 17.

15. Laurie Beth Jones, *Jesus, CEO* (New York: Hyperion, 1995), 78.

16. Smith, *Empowering Ministry*, 145.

17. Ibid., 147.

18. Collins, *Good to Great*, 12.

19. Jones, *Jesus, CEO*, 24.

20. Woods, *Better than Success*, xiii.

21. Ettinger and Neinast, *The Long and Winding Road*, 31.

22. Carl F. George, *Prepare Your Church for the Future* (Grand Rapids: Fleming H. Revell, 1992), 85.

23. Warren, *The Purpose-Driven Church*, 208.

24. Ibid., 17.

25. George, *Prepare Your Church for the Future*, 69.

26. Jones, *Jesus, CEO*, 4.

27. Smith, *Empowering Ministry*, 27.

28. Collins, *Good to Great*, 12.

29. George Barna, *The Habits of Highly Effective Churches* (Ventura, Calif.: Regal Books, 1999), 158.

30. Watchman Nee, *Spiritual Authority* (New York: Christian Fellowship Publishers, 1972), 47.

31. Blackaby and King, *Experiencing God*, 168.

Bibliography

The Doctrine and Discipline of the African Methodist Episcopal Church 2004, Nashville: AMEC *Sunday School Union,* 2005.

Arn, Charles. *How to Start a New Service: Your Church Can Reach New People.* Grand Rapids: Baker, 1997.

Barna, George. *Evangelism That Works: How to Reach Changing Generations with the Unchanging Gospel.* Ventura, Calif.: Regal Books, 1995.

———. *The Frog in the Kettle: What Christians Need to Know about Life in the Year 2000.* Ventura, Calif.: Regal Books, 1990.

———. *The Habits of Highly Effective Churches: What It Takes to Have a Transforming Ministry.* Ventura, Calif.: Regal Books, 1999.

———. *Marketing the Church.* Colorado Springs: NavPress, 1988.

Blackaby, Henry T., and Claude V. King. *Experiencing God: Knowing and Doing the Will of God.* Nashville: Lifeway Press, 1990.

Blanchard, Ken, John P. Carlos, and W. Alan Randolph. *Empowerment Takes More Than a Minute.* San Francisco: Berrett-Koehler Publishers, 1996.

Blanchard, Kenneth H., Dana Gaines Robinson, and James C. Robinson. *Zap the Gaps: Target Higher Performance and Achieve It!* New York: William Morrow, 2002.

Callahan, Kennon L. *Twelve Keys to an Effective Church.* San Francisco: Harper & Row, 1983.

Collins, Jim. *Good to Great: Why Some Companies Make the Leap — and Others Don't.* New York: HarperBusiness, 2001.

Ettinger, Thomas C., and Helen R. Neinast. *The Long and Winding Road: A Spiritual Guide for Baby Boomers.* Nashville: Dimensions, 1998.

Flake, Floyd H., Elaine McCollins Flake, and Edwin C. Reed, *African American Church Management Handbook,* Valley Forge, Pa.: Judson Press, 2005.

George, Carl F. *Prepare Your Church for the Future.* Grand Rapids: Fleming H. Revell, 1992.

Johnson, Spencer, M.D. *Who Moved My Cheese? An Amazing Way to Deal with Change in Your Work and in Your Life.* New York: G. P. Putnam Sons, 1998.

Jones, Laurie Beth. *Jesus, CEO: Using Ancient Wisdom for Visionary Leadership.* New York: Hyperion, 1995.

Massey, Floyd, Jr., and Samuel Berry McKinney. *Church Administration in the Black Perspective: A Look at the Operation Of Black Baptist Churches.* Valley Forge, Pa.: Judson Press, 1976.

McIntosh, Gary L. *Staff Your Church for Growth: Building Team Ministry in the 21st Century.* Grand Rapids: Baker, 2000.

Nee, Watchman. *Spiritual Authority.* New York: Christian Fellowship Publishers, 1972.

Nelson, Alan, and Stan Toler. *The Five-Star Church: Helping Your Church Provide the Highest Level of Service to God and His People.* Ventura, Calif.: Regal Books, 1999.

Ott, E. Stanley. *Twelve Dynamic Shifts for Transforming Your Church.* Grand Rapids: William Eerdmans Publishing Company, 2002.

Richardson, Alan. *A Dictionary of Christian Theology.* Philadelphia: Westminster Press, 1969.

Smith, Donald P. *Empowering Ministry: Ways to Grow in Effectiveness.* Louisville: Westminster John Knox Press, 1996.

Toffler, Alvin. *Future Shock.* New York: Bantam Books, 1970.

Warren, Rick. *The Purpose-Driven Church.* Grand Rapids: Zondervan, 1995.

Woods, C. Jeff. *Better Than Success: 8 Principles of Faithful Leadership.* Valley Forge, Pa.: Judson Press, 1989.